Rock Hunting in Texas

Where to go and what to look for!

Enjoy the best of Texas with these Lone Star Books:

The Alamo and Other Texas Missions to Remember

Amazing Texas Monuments and Museums

Backroads of Texas

Beachcomber's Guide to Gulf Coast Marine Life

The Best of Texas Festivals

Bicycling in Texas

Camper's Guide to Texas Parks, Lakes, and Forests/2nd Edition

From Texas Kitchens

Great Hometown Restaurants of Texas

A Guide to Fishing in Texas

A Guide to Historic Texas Inns and Hotels/2nd Edition

A Guide to Hunting in Texas

A Guide to Texas Lakes

A Guide to Texas Rivers and Streams

Hiking and Backpacking Trails of Texas/2nd Edition

A Line on Texas

Rock Hunting in Texas

Texas Birds: Where They Are and How to Find Them

Texas—Family Style

Traveling Texas Borders

Unsung Heroes of Texas

Why Stop? A Guide to Texas Historical Roadside Markers/2nd Edition

Rock Hunting in Texas

Where to go and what to look for!

Margaret Gronberg
Linda Nutting

Lone Star Books
A Division of Gulf Publishing Company
Houston, Texas

Library of Congress Cataloging-in-Publication Data

Gronberg, Margaret.
Rock hunting in Texas.

Includes index.
1. Rocks—Collectors and collecting—Texas.
2. Geology—Texas. I. Nutting, Linda. II. Title.
QE445.T4G76 1986 552′.0075′09764
85-27021

ISBN 0-88415-786-5

CONTENTS

INTRODUCTION

For years, Texans have taken pride in their state and its unique features. One of the most interesting features, available for the enjoyment of everyone is the wide range of rocks for collecting. The state's vastly differing terrain provides the amateur collector with everything from blue topaz (the state gemstone) to fossils. Some are beautiful in their specimen form, while others can be cut and polished for jewelry. No rockhunter will be disappointed in his searches.

Throughout the history of rockhunting, most information regarding the best locations for finds has been passed from one person to another by word of mouth. There is a network of gem and mineral clubs throughout the state whose members share a passion for rocks. They offer excellent opportunities for the beginning rockhunter and frequently organize field trips, sometimes to areas inaccessible to the average collector. Club members will usually pass along helpful hints as well.

The purpose of this guide is to give you an idea of which rocks are found in the state, where you can find them, and how to identify them. Photographs are included to aid you in your search. The book divides the state into four regions for easier site location and provides area maps for further detail concerning site access.

The collector must remember to read the details about each area before venturing in and removing rocks. There are two reasons for this: first, some areas are designated as national or state parks where collecting is forbidden. Second, some areas are private property where the owners make a portion of their income from fees paid by rockhunters. Remember this, and you won't be surprised when the owner asks for a few dollars. If you are fortunate enough to know someone who owns property in an area, that is a good place to start. And because other collectors haven't been there ahead of you, specimens will be more abundant. Some of our most successful hunting has been on private property not open to the public.

At the end of each section we have included a list of nearby points of interest which you might enjoy visiting.

Keep the book handy when taking trips around the state and wherever you are, chances are good an interesting collecting site will not be far away. Have fun discovering the rocks of Texas.

PREPARATION AND EQUIPMENT

Rockhunting does take some preparation. Minor injuries can be prevented by following a few guidelines. First, wear the proper clothing. Wear long pants, (preferably jeans), a long-sleeved shirt and sturdy shoes with socks. Shorts and sandals are not the correct attire for rockhunting. Much of the best rockhunting is in overgrown, brushy areas along stream beds where branches can be hazardous to bare limbs. Second, bring water. A gallon jug can provide water for drinking, as well as for splashing on over-heated skin. Third, carry a snake bite kit. People aren't often bitten, but when someone is, the nearest doctor or hospital might be miles away. Fourth, don't forget personal necessities.

You will need the following basic equipment:

1. Prospector's hammer
2. Safety goggles
3. Hand loupe or magnifying glass
4. Leather or gardening gloves
5. Heavy duty plastic bags (zip tops work well)
6. Stick on labels or tape (to identify find locations)

ROCKS AND MINERALS

Rocks and minerals are often discussed as though they are the same thing, but that is not the case. Let us begin with their structure.

All matter is made up of chemical elements. Some examples of elements are: sulfur, gold, carbon, silicon, oxygen, and mercury. There are over one hundred documented elements. Sometimes these elements come together and form inorganic compounds called minerals. Each mineral has its own chemical composition, growth structure (crystal system) and density (specific gravity). These features help identify the material. Occasionally, a single element can be called a mineral, too. When it is produced by nature with its own distinct mineralogical properties, it is called *native*. One often sees the term *native silver* applied to a specimen of silver brought directly out of the ground.

Rocks, on the other hand, are composed of several minerals in combination.

TYPES OF ROCKS

Three broad classifications of rock are: igneous, sedimentary, and metamorphic.

1. IGNEOUS rocks result from the cooling of molten rock (magma). Magma spewing from a volcano is what we know as lava. As the magma cools, different minerals crystallize in combination sometimes making it difficult to separate them.

Igneous rocks that form above the earth's surface are called extrusive. If they form under the surface, they are called intrusive. Extrusive rock is that which is no longer being formed, and can be seen in areas of extinct volcanoes around the state. Intrusive rock can be seen on the earth's surface in several locations, due to erosion and uplift (the earth pushing upward from below).

2. **SEDIMENTARY** rocks are composed of sediments or weathered minerals of all kinds. The forces of wind and water cause rocks to break apart and dissolve, thereby producing the finer-grained sediments. Sands and soils are a result of the erosion of mineral material.

Large pebbles (gravel) of differing mineral material are sometimes consolidated by a naturally occurring cement such as dissolved calcium carbonate to form sandstone or shale.

Sedimentary rocks can also form by the precipitation of dissolved material from a solution. Rock material that has dissolved in water will often come out of solution and cause sediments. An example is the crusty deposit frequently seen in water pipes or tea kettles. Some types of limestone form this way.

3. **METAMORPHIC** rocks, as the name implies, have undergone a change from their original state.

Heat, pressure and fluids (liquids and gasses) produce changes from below the earth's surface. As rocks are deposited on top of one another, the older, more deeply buried rocks are subjected to greater heat and pressure. This can change shale (sedimentary) into slate, limestone (sedimentary) into marble and granite (igneous) into gneiss. Changes can also occur if magma moves through rocks exposing them to liquids and gasses as well as heat and pressure. Or rock changing can be caused by "mountain building" where the movement of the earth's surface creates the heat and pressure necessary to metamorphize rock.

Identifying Minerals and Rocks

It is possible for even the amateur to identify rocks and minerals using information about the physical and chemical properties. In many cases this can be done by simple visual examination, or by the application of very basic mineralogical tests. For the identification process there are ten features that are readily observable in each rock. They are: crystallization, color, transparency, luster, hardness, specific gravity, effervescence, streak, fracture, and cleavage. You may find that you want to take notes on a particularly difficult specimen and then ask an expert to identify it.

Crystallization. Minerals form according to nature's plan for the orderly arrangement of the atoms. This is called the *crystal system*. The outer shape that the crystal forms is called the *crystal habit*. The crystal system is not always evident from the outward appearance. A crystal may form in such microscopic sizes that it cannot be seen with the naked eye. Such material is described as massive. Agate is a result of the massive formation of cryptocrystalline quartz.

The experienced rockhunter can sometimes use the shape of the crystal or crystal system to help identify the material. These shapes may be cubic, hexagonal, tetragonal, triclinic or monoclinic.

Color. This is often noted subconsciously by the observer, but it should be remembered that color can sometimes vary in the same material due to impurities changing or masking the true color.

Transparency. Transparency is a measure of how much light can pass through a material. Light and objects are visible through *transparent* material, while only light is visible through *translucent* material. *Opaque* material transmits no light.

Luster. The measure of reflection of light from a surface is called *luster*. Lusters are either adamantine (diamond-like), pearly, dull, waxy (silky), vitreous (glassy), metallic or submetallic. The luster of a material is determined simply by visual examination and does not require a trained eye.

Hardness. *Hardness* is defined as the resistance of a substance to scratching or abrasion. The hardness of a rock or mineral is assigned a number from one to ten on the Mohs scale. To determine hardness, the material can be scratched with objects of a known hardness. Some common tools for measuring hardness are fingernails (2+), copper pennies (3), pocket knives (5+), pieces of glass (5½) and steel files (6½).

Examples of each level of hardness are given below.

1. Talc
2. Gypsum
3. Calcite
4. Fluorite
5. Apatite
6. Orthoclase (feldspar)
7. Quartz
8. Topaz
9. Corundum
10. Diamond

Specific Gravity. *Specific gravity* is the density of a material. It is the ratio of the weight of a substance to that of an equal volume of water.

We have all heard the trick question, "Which weighs more, a ton of bricks or a ton of feathers?" Of course, they weigh the same, but think about the volume. How much space would a ton of feathers take up as compared to a ton of bricks? Naturally, the feathers have a lesser density so they would take up a greater volume. The same principle can be applied in rockhunting. The most common method of determining specific gravity is the "heft" method, where the material is simply tossed in the hand to feel the impact when it hits the palm. Of course, this is a very inexact method, but can be a helpful indicator when combined with other features. Another method of determining specific gravity is by using heavy liquids. Materials are dropped into liquids of a pre-determined specific gravity and their reaction noted. This is a test used by experienced rock hunters and gemologists. A third method requires special equipment such as a diamond balance scale and apparatus to weigh the material in air and water. This is usually not necessary for the amateur.

Effervescence. This is the reaction of a mineral to the application of a small amount of diluted hydrochloric acid. If a mineral contains a carbonate, it will fizz when several drops of the acid are applied. This should be done very carefully as the acid can burn and stain the skin.

Streak. *Streak* is the mark made by rubbing a mineral across a streak plate. The streak color is sometimes very indicative of certain minerals and helpful in its identification. This plate is tile or porcelain with a dull surface and has a hardness of about seven on the Mohs scale. If the mineral tested has a greater hardness, then a small amount of the material will have to be crushed and the color observed.

Fracture. The described visual appearance of a material when broken is termed *fracture*. It is a break in a direction other than along a cleavage plane (see Cleavage below). It can be described as conchoidal (shell-like), even, uneven or splintery.

The broken lip of a bottle exhibits *conchoidal* fracture. *Even fracture* is a smooth, even break that shows no irregularity. *Uneven fracture* is that shown by the edge of broken pottery. *Splintery fracture* is visible in a broken piece of wood.

Cleavage. *Cleavage* is a property possessed by some stones and minerals wherein the material splits along a certain plane that is atomically weak. It can be compared with wood which splits easily along the grain. When cleavage occurs, a flat, sheer surface remains.

ROCKS AND MINERALS AS GEMSTONES

Occasionally, stones are found of such quality that they can be cut, polished and worn as gemstones. In order to be a gem, a stone must possess certain qualities.

First, it must have sufficient *beauty* to be significant for wear as adornment. Naturally, this is often in the eye of the beholder.

Second, the stone must be *wearable*. In other words, it must be hard enough to take a polish, and durable enough so that the wearer can get several years' wear out of it. If a stone is too soft to hold a polish after several months wear or breaks easily when struck, then the wearer is going to be disappointed with the piece.

Third, the stone should have *rarity*. The more rare a stone, the more valuable it is. If you have found a stone that has occurred in some rare formation or color, then it has added value. Even though most of the stones found in Texas are not extremely rare when compared with others around the world, some unique formations have occurred that are very interesting.

CUTTING STONES

In your travels of the state, if you find a stone that you think is worthy of being cut and polished, then don't damage it any more than is necessary to free it from the surrounding material. That way, maximum yield can be realized when the material is cut.

To find someone to cut a stone for you, contact the nearest gem and mineral club or a local rock shop. Keep in mind that it may cost more to cut the stone than it will be worth as a gemstone. However, don't let this stop you if the cost is not out of your budget and you will enjoy wearing your ''find.''

There are two basic styles of stone cutting. One is *faceting*, where the stone is cut with small triangular sections, a flat top and a cone shaped bottom. The other is called *en cabochon*, with a flat bottom and a domed top. Most of the stones found in Texas will lend themselves to being cut en cabochon.

IN SUMMARY

Now you are ready to hunt for rocks. You have some idea what you will need to find the rocks, how they are formed, and how to recognize what they are. Armed with this information, we intend to lead you across the state and into areas where the rockhunting experience will be a satisfying one.

GEOLOGIC TIME CHART

Throughout the book, when we speak of a rock formation occurring during a certain geologic period, we are speaking of millions of years ago. Therefore, use the chart below in order to pinpoint the geologic chronology that created a certain rock.

Geologic Time Chart

Era	Epoch	Period	Life Forms	Years Ago
		Recent		
Cenozoic	Quarternary	Pleistocene	Man	3 Million
	Tertiary	Piliocene		
		Miocene	Apes	
		Oligocene	Birds	
		Eocene	Mammals	
		Paleocene		70 Million
		Cretaceous		
Mesozoic	Secondary	Jurassic	Reptiles	
		Triassic		250 Million
		Permian	Land Plants	
		Pennsylvanian	Insects	
		Mississippian	Amphibians	
Paleozoic	Primary	Devonian	Fishes	
		Silurian	Marine Plants	
		Ordovician	Shell Fish	
		Cambrian	Scavengers	600 Million
Archeozoic-			Jellyfish	
Proterozoic		Pre-	Corals	
		Cambrian	Algae	
			Bacteria	4000 Million

TEXAS: A GEOLOGICAL PERSPECTIVE

Texas is a large state and the geology of it varies greatly, so we have chosen to divide the state into four regions. We have endeavored to make the divisions roughly along geological boundaries. In each region some areas provide bountiful rock-hunting potential while others are somewhat scarce by comparison. Therefore, large areas may not necessarily offer greater collecting potential than small areas.

The history of the earth's formation is reflected in the exposed surfaces around the state. As the earth's crust formed, starting some three billion years ago, the sea played its part by advancing and receding, all the while depositing lime bearing sands, silts and muds. This material was altered by heat, pressure, and chemical processes to form the limestone that now makes up major portions of the state's surface.

This book is divided into chapters representing the rough geologic regions above. For a detailed map of Texas' surface geology, see page 85.

An inland sea that covered the northwestern half of the state left sediments that give evidence to changes in conditions beginning some 500 to 600 million years ago. Westward flowing rivers left vast amounts of mud and sand that created great deltas with limestone banks. Vegetation of this period was dominated by huge ferns. Much of the oil and gas produced in the state originates in this rock. The slowly drying sea also left deposits of salt which are still mined.

Some 300 million years ago, the only sea left was limited to what we know as the panhandle and far west areas of the state. The limestone reefs that formed were composed of the skeletons of marine animals. (This formation is similar to the Great Barrier Reef of Australia.) Its most spectacular exposure is El Capitan, the highest point in the state at 8,751 ft above sea level. El Capitan is located in Guadalupe Park in far west Texas.

Shortly thereafter (in geologic time), 50 million years later, Texas was largely a land area. Changes that occurred in this period include the subsiding of the Gulf Coast land masses with seas advancing from the east. The westerly inland sea was now essentially gone and the rocks of west and central Texas were deposited by rivers and wind. In the eastern part of the state the sea was retreating and advancing leaving thick layers of salt where the water had been trapped and evaporated. Salt domes formed when this salt was squeezed up under high pressure and temperature.

Then came the great floods of 180 million years ago. The lime muds now make up the limestone and marl of the Hill Country, central Texas and the plains of southwest Texas. It was at this time that the dinosaurs flourished. It was also at this time that great disturbances in the earth's crust occurred. Folding and faulting resulted in the creation of the Rocky Mountains in far west Texas and the Llano-Burnet Uplift in central Texas.

More recent times, 80 to 3 million years ago, have seen the receding of the Gulf of Mexico to its current status. This retreat has left the coastal plains covered in deposits of sand and mud 50,000 feet thick.

The ice ages of three million years ago did not reach Texas, but they caused the sea level to drop. As the ice melted, flooding left large areas of sand and gravel covering parts of the state.

It was not until two million years ago that man made his first appearance on earth and 20,000 years ago that Texas was first inhabited by man. So it is only recently, in geologic terms, that man has been in Texas. Even the most boastful of Texans must be humbled by the fact that he is a newcomer to the earth's surface.

Section 1

CENTRAL TEXAS

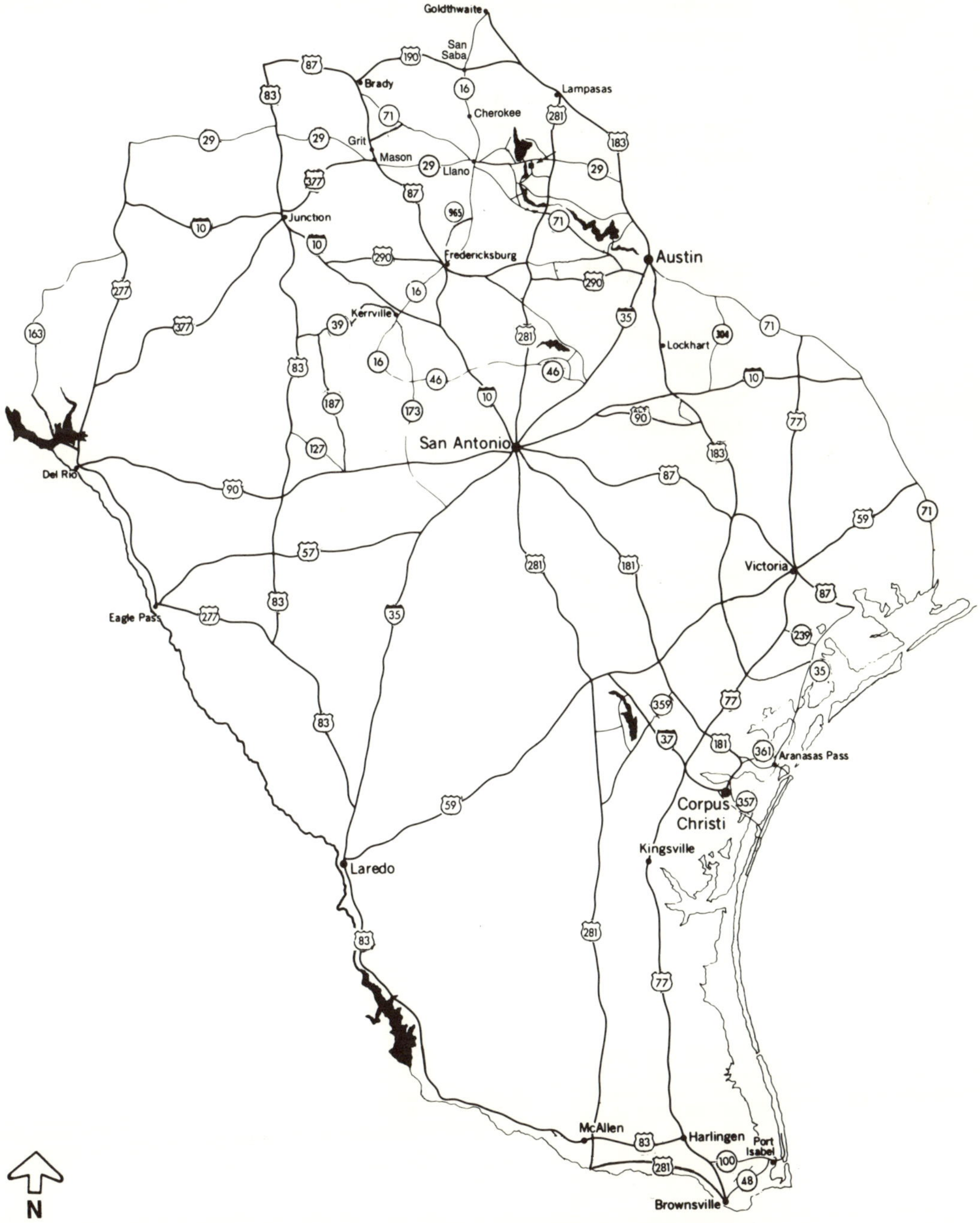

INTRODUCTION

This area is bordered on the east by the Balcones Fault Zone, on the south by the Rio Grande River, on the west by the Edwards Plateau, and on the north by the great plains regions of the Grand Prairie and North Central Plains. In more familiar terms, the area can be approximately defined as that land enclosed by the perimeter cities of Austin, Corpus Christi, Brownsville, Del Rio, San Angelo, and Killeen.

In the Hill Country of the upper central portion of this section, are found the most interesting rock formations. In geological terms, this area is called the Llano Uplift and dates from the Precambrian period. Much of the material is igneous rock, having been formed by the intrusion of magma into older metamorphic rocks that used to form the surface (and still do in some places). The area is covered with the domes of granite that pushed their way to the earth's surface. These rock formations are called outcroppings.

ASBESTOS

This is the name given to several minerals that form in slender fibers. The most widely known type of asbestos can be pulled apart into soft strings and is used industrially as cloth for such things as fireproof suits, gloves and theater curtains.

The fibers are actually separations along the two perfect cleavage planes. It is green or gray with a white streak and soft enough to be scratched with a copper penny.

The kind of asbestos most often used by industry, chrysotile asbestos, is found in metamorphic rock in northwestern Blanco County, but its fibers are not sufficiently fine or flexible enough to use for fireproof cloth.

BARITE

The barium sulfate mineral that has a glassy or pearly luster is called barite. It can be white, brownish, bluish, yellowish or reddish and has a white streak. Its distinctive qualities include a high specific gravity, being heavy for a non-metallic mineral and three directions of cleavage.

When barite occurs in crystal form, it is flat or prism-shaped. However, in Texas, barite is most often deposited as masses in sedimentary rock. In Gillespie and Llano Counties it can also be found in metamorphic rock.

CALCITE

Calcite is a mineral made up of the elements calcium, carbon and oxygen forming calcium carbonate. This mineral is extremely common and often occurs mixed with other minerals to form rocks. Alone in pure form, it exhibits large crystals with very distinct crystal faces.

Calcite most often occurs as white, being either transparent or translucent with perfect cleavage in three directions. It will effervesce with a few drops of a dilute solution of hydrochloric acid and can be scratched with a copper penny.

Calcium carbonate also takes the form of stalagmites and stalactites in cave formations. Stalactites occur when water, heavily laden with dissolved calcium carbonate, flows over the edge of a rock. Over a period of centuries, as the water evaporates, the calcite deposits itself on the surface and hardens forming what appears to be an icicle. Stalagmites form when drops of the same type of water fall continually on a surface and slowly build upwards. Flowstone forms when this water seeps through an opening in the ground and flows outward.

These cave formations can be seen in central Texas at the Inner Space Caverns just north of Austin. For a small fee you can wander through the formations that began millions of years ago.

Calcite is usually white, transparent or translucent, with perfect cleavage in three directions.

CASSITERITE

Cassiterite is tin dioxide and the primary source of tin. It is transparent or translucent and occurs as black, brown, gray, reddish brown or yellowish brown. It is very heavy and is too hard to be scratched with a knife.

A simple chemical test will identify the material, however. Place the suspected cassiterite in a jar with a small amount of dilute hydrochloric acid and a small piece of the metal zinc. If the material becomes covered with a pale gray coating, then it is cassiterite.

Cassiterite is not often found in crystalline form in Texas. As the tin-bearing fluid, given off by partially cooled magma, seeped through the granite, it carried tin into the cracks. Therefore, it is usually found in conjunction with granite or other volcanic rock, most notably in the Llano Uplift, Mason County area.

CORAL, OPALIZED

Fossil producing areas around the state occasionally produce such unique items as opalized coral. This occurs when the structure of the coral is completely taken over by opal and is technically no longer coral. However, it still retains the coral form. This is called a pseudomorph, or false form.

Since coral is an organic life form, it naturally occurred where the terrain used to be covered with water. Such an area is in the central part of Texas where crinoids are also found. In prehistoric times, this area was completely covered by sea and held abundant life.

The coral is revealed as a black or dark gray radiating circle embedded in white limestone. (See FOSSILS.)

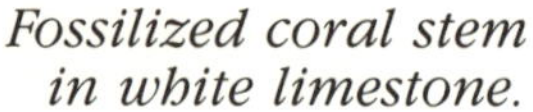

Fossilized coral stem in white limestone.

FELDSPAR

Feldspar is the name given to a group of similar non-metallic minerals, called aluminum silicates. The different varieties are created by the addition of one or more of the following: potassium, sodium, calcium or barium. Those occurring in Texas are *albite* (sodium-aluminum silicate) and *orthoclase* and *microcline* (potassium-aluminum silicate).

These minerals are found in a range of colors including white, cream, red, brown, yellow, blue, gray or green and have

Large feldspar crystal granite.

a white streak. The material is fairly hard and cannot be scratched with a pocket knife, and has two distinct directions of cleavage.

Feldspars are found with igneous rocks, often mixed with other minerals as well. Granite is a good example of this. Individual, well-formed pinkish crystals have been found in Mason and Llano counties of central Texas.

A gem form of feldspar, moonstone, has been found in very small quantities in the state. It can be colorless, to light pinkish brown and has a phenomenon called adularescence, a floating, billowy blue light when cut en cabochon.

FLINT

This is actually a quartz material and probably one of the most widely known stones in existence. When quartz forms in crystals too small to see with the naked eye, it is called cryptocrystalline quartz or chalcedony (pronounced Kal-SED-on-e). Flint is a hard, smooth chalcedony material that is translucent and occurs in white, black, gray, brown or pink.

Indian arrowheads and hand axes made of this material can be found in creek and river gravels. Flint is also commonly found with limestone in this area of Texas.

Flint hand ax.

Fossilized shell in limestone.

Fossilized coral stem.

FOSSILS

The remains or imprint of an organism that has been buried by natural causes and preserved by the earth's crust is what we know as a fossil. A great deal can be learned about the flora and fauna throughout the history of this planet by studying fossil remains of plants and animals.

Most fossils are found in sedimentary rocks and occasionally occur in igneous or metamorphic rocks. Only a very small portion of those organisms that lived in prehistoric times have been preserved for us in fossil form.

For a fossil to form, three qualifications must be met. First of all, the organism must possess hard parts, such as bone, teeth or shell. Second, the remains must escape immediate destruction after death by decay, weathering or damage. Third, the organism must be rapidly buried in a material that will retard decomposition. Limy mud, sand, volcano ash, tar and ice are all suitable preserving materials because they can quickly surround the organism and prevent the hard parts from decaying.

Let's pretend for a moment that we are two-inch prehistoric fish swimming around in the ocean several million years ago. Perhaps, at a very young age, we are beset by disaster and die. Slowly, our body floats down, down to the sea bed where a layer of sand gently covers us. Our body begins to be covered with many layers of sand and the pressure of the sand and water begins to harden the sea bottom into stone. After millions of years of pressure and maybe even some heat from underground volcanoes, the rock holding our remains forms into what we see today: stone with our fossilized remains preserved for millenniums.

Fossils are found throughout the entire state, both of plants and animals, but there are several general rules to remember in collecting. They are more likely to be found in limestone, shale and sandstone type materials than in igneous or metamorphic rock.

FOSSILIZED CRINOIDS IN LIMESTONE

In the central part of Texas, a great deal of the rock material is limestone. Limestone is a sedimentary rock formed from the constant erosion of rocks into a fine powdery material, often dissolved in hard water. The powdery material settles and through the process of deposition and hardening, stone forms.

The area around Austin has an abundance of limestone and it has been used for many years as building material. It is even called "Austin Stone" and is a beautiful creamy-yellow color.

Crinoids are sea animals that are shaped more like plants than animals. A crinoid possesses what appears to be a floral cup,

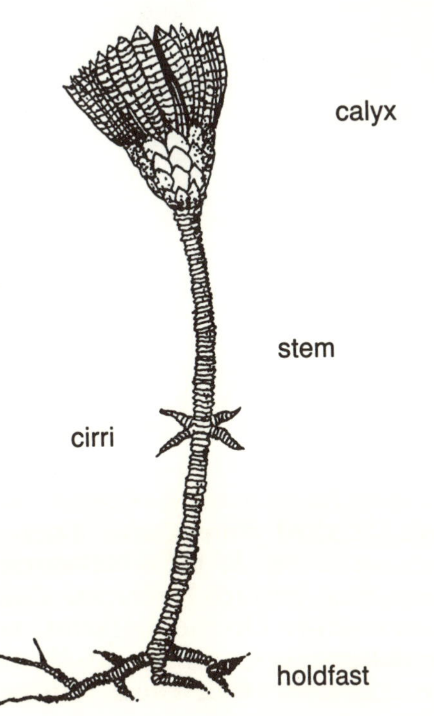

Crinoids look like plants, but are actually sea animals.

stem and root. This is actually the *calyx* and *holdfast,* respectively, of the invertebrate. Most of what remains in fossil form today is the stem portion since the calyx is soft material and more prone to decay. Being gregarious animals, these "sea lilies" lived together in large numbers and can therefore be found in abundant quantities in this area.

Crinoid stem in white limestone.

Crinoids in white limestone.

FOSSILIZED TURRITELLA IN LIMESTONE

Turritella is a tertiary gastropod, a freshwater shellfish of long spiralled cone shape. These shellfish were prolific when the central area of Texas was covered with sea during the lower Cretaceous period. Today, the shells of these marine animals remain fossilized in the limestone of central Texas. Usually when the material is found, the fossils are so completely embedded in the limestone that they cannot be separated from it. The creamy base color of limestone is accented with an abundance of shells, and when cut, is a beautiful ornamental stone. This material has been quarried for building purposes.

GARNET

Garnet is the name given to a group of minerals so similar that laboratory tests have to be used to tell them apart. The ones most commonly found in Texas are *almandite* (iron-aluminum silicate) and *grossularite* (calcium-aluminum silicate). Almandite is dark red or brown-red; grossularite is pale yellow-green, brownish-yellow, cinnamon brown or red.

Texas garnet is usually not transparent enough to be of gem quality. It occurs as translucent to nearly opaque with stubby or rounded crystals scattered throughout metamorphic and igneous rock. However, on those rare occasions when the material does occur in transparent form, it can be fashioned into a gemstone.

Garnet is found in the Llano Uplift area in Mason and Llano Counties.

GNEISS

Pronounced "nice," this is a metamorphic rock that forms in parallel, light and dark bands. It must possess these bands in order to be gneiss and can be formed either as an igneous rock or as a sedimentary rock upon which the earth's heat, fluids and pressures acted.

Most gneiss has the same components as granite (quartz and feldspar) and is of the same hardness. Some central Texas gneiss is made up of sandstone and is pink in color. Another type is altered igneous rock which is gray in color.

Gneiss is found in the Llano Uplift area in Gillespie and Blanco Counties.

Gneiss, which has parallel light and dark bands, can be formed from igneous or sedimentary rock.

Large-grained granite, one of Texas' most abundant rocks.

GRANITE

This lovely material is one of Texas' most abundant rocks. It is composed of quartz and feldspar and possibly hornblende or mica. The pink color of the famous central Texas granite is imparted by the pink feldspar it contains. Our own state capitol building is made of this material.

Granite is intrusive igneous rock, molten material that cooled very slowly below the earth's surface and then pushed its way upward. The slow cooling created the large grains that can be easily seen in the material.

In many areas of the state and particularly throughout central Texas, large outcroppings of pink granite are visible from the road. Most of the material is on fenced, private property, but quite a bit can be found along the roadside.

Its abundance makes it of great commercial value and it is quarried for building purposes.

GRAPHITE

Graphite is made up of a single element, carbon, the same element that crystallizes to form diamonds. It is a steel gray or black color, not heavy and extremely soft. It cleaves perfectly in one direction and easily flakes into small pieces that have a greasy feel.

It occurs as sheet-like layers or compact masses and is sometimes mixed with clay and only rarely occurs in six-sided flat crystals.

Graphite is found in very old Precambrian schist rock that is now on the surface. It is believed that this was once ancient sedimentary rock that contained organic matter. Tremendous heat and pressure long ago altered these rocks, changing the organic material into what we now know as graphite.

It has many important industrial uses. Combined with clay, it is used for pencil lead. Mixed with oil or grease, it is used as a lubricant. One of the most important graphite mines in the country is located in the Clear Creek area of northwest Burnet County in the Llano Uplift area.

LIMESTONE

It can be said that limestone is the glue of the mineral world, for it is the major component that cements other rocks together. The material itself can be used in several different ways that have practical purposes. Chalk, for instance, is a limestone. It is soft, white and very fine-grained. Another type of limestone is lithographic limestone, used for printing.

The major component of limestone is calcium carbonate in very tiny grains. These settle into a limy mud that forms sedimentary rock. The finer the mud, the finer grained the limestone will be. Anything that falls into this mud will also be formed into sedimentary rock under nature's pressure and heat.

Dense, fine grained limestone is quarried for building purposes. The Central Texas area produces some beautiful pink, gray and black limestone, sometimes embedded with fossils.

Pink limestone is characteristic of central Texas.

LLANITE

Llanite is a type of pink granite found nowhere else in the world except Llano County. Its combination of tiny grains of blue agate mixed with pink feldspar and quartz make the material unique and prized by collectors. There are many areas in

Llanite, a type of pink granite, is found in only one place in the world, Llano County, Texas.

the county where the material can be found. It can be seen in outcroppings along the side of some highways and was first discovered when road cuts were made for highways.

MARBLE

The metamorphic rock which contains mostly calcite or dolomite that has been changed by extreme heat and pressure from below the earth's surface causing the calcite and dolomite mineral grains to re-crystallize is called marble.

It can be almost any color, depending on the minerals that occur with the calcite or dolomite. Additionally, it can be uniform in color, or banded, spotted or streaked. Pure white marble is made up of only calcite or dolomite. If it contains graphite, it is gray or black; manganese oxides and hematite cause a pink, brown or red color.

Commercially, Llano County marble has been quarried and used for monuments and building stones.

OPAL

Opal is a non-crystalline or amorphous silicate material. Since it does not form in a crystal system, it is found in veins that fill the cracks of other material. As silicate bearing water moves through a substance (rocks, wood, coral, shells) the opal is deposited on that substance and slowly fills the pores or cracks. In some cases, the opal takes over the structure of the material, but not its form. Consequently, we have opalized wood and shells that retain the shape and structure of the original material, but are now opal.

Opal can occur in many different colors, but is most often found with a white or jelly-like base either transparent or trans-

Common opal on white limestone.

lucent. Lucky is the collector that has found precious opal in Texas. This is opal with a strong play of color. Play of color is created when light reflects from the trapped water molecules in the silicate. Opal with no play of color is called common opal.

We found several good examples of common opal in conjunction with crinoids in limestone and opalized coral. All were white base, translucent and formed thin veins in the limestone material.

PYRITE

Pyrite is a bright yellow metallic mineral, iron disulfide. Crystals of this mineral are often cubic in shape, but also can be found as granular or compact masses in igneous, metamorphic or sedimentary rock.

Pyrite has much the same look as gold, and was once so often mistaken for it that it was given the name "Fool's Gold." It can be distinguished from gold by its hardness, since gold can be easily scratched with a knife and pyrite can't. Also, pyrite is brittle and breaks easily, whereas gold does not.

Its iron content means that it will alter easily and change color.

In this area of the state, pyrite most often occurs in veins of other substances such as quartz or granite. It crystallizes in the cubic shape or some distortion thereof.

QUARTZ

The silicon dioxide which is one of the most common minerals is called *quartz.* It can be found in many different forms, shapes and colors around the state of Texas. In its purest form it is a transparent colorless hexagonally shaped crystal *(rock crys-*

Pure quartz is transparent and colorless, but impurities can make it white, brown, yellow, blue, pink, and even black.

tal), but impurities create different colors such as white, brown, yellow, blue, pink and even black.

Throughout central Texas quartz is found in conjunction with other rocks. We found much milky quartz with llanite and granite.

One of the most prized of all quartz finds is *smoky quartz* (often incorrectly called smoky topaz). It is found as weathered, transparent or translucent pale to dark brown hexagonally shaped crystals. This material is often cut for gem use and is hard enough (hardness 7) to take a fine polish and wears very well.

A great deal of this has been found along with topaz in the stream beds of the central Texas hill country. Hardy collectors have found good specimens through a process of digging and sifting the dirt and sand of stream beds.

SANDSTONE

Sand is grains of uncemented fragments of weathered rocks and minerals that are between 1/16 millimeter and 2 millimeters

Desert rose, weathered sandstone.

in size. Most sand is made up of grains of quartz since it does not weather away easily.

When the grains of sand are cemented together by nature they make the sedimentary rock, *sandstone*. The cement can be calcite, quartz, chalcedony, opal or the iron oxides, limonite and hematite. This cementing material is responsible in large part for the resulting color of the sandstone.

Sandstone is formed when mineral-laden water moves through grains of sand and comes out of solution, cementing the grains together.

Sandstone is found on the surface in the Llano Uplift area and is used commercially for building material.

SERPENTINE

Serpentine can be either a mineral or a rock. The mineral is a hydrous magnesium silicate in either a fibrous or layered formation. It is brownish-green in color and has a smooth or waxy luster. It is soft enough to be scratched with a pocket knife.

In the Llano area of central Texas there is a major deposit of serpentine known as the Coal Creek mass. It spans the Blanco-Gillespie county line in the far northern part of these counties. It is not easily seen on the surface.

This material is used extensively for terrazzo flooring. Small pieces of serpentine are mixed with a cement and then ground smooth and flat when it has dried. Slabs of serpentine are also used for building materials.

TOPAZ

A great deal has been written about the occurrence of blue topaz in Mason County. After all, it has been declared the state stone. The material that occurs in Texas is such a light blue that it should be called pale blue, and most of it is really colorless. If you keep that in mind while looking for it, you won't be disappointed.

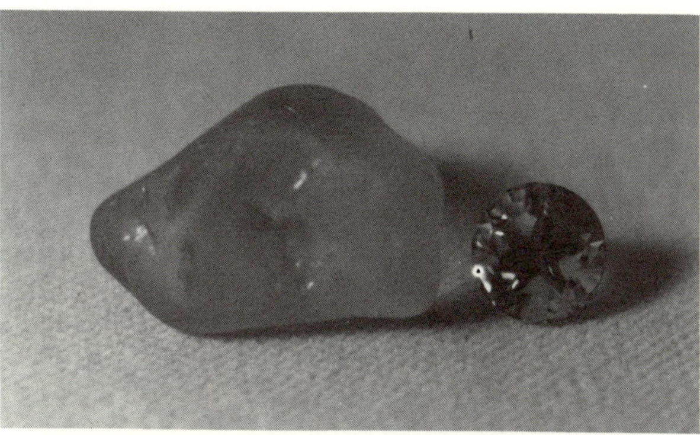

Blue topaz, rough and Lone Star cut.

Some helpful pointers should aid the hunting for blue topaz. The material will have been weathered and will look frosty or dull. It has perfect cleavage as evidenced by the sheer edge of the pebble. This helps to distinguish it from quartz which also occurs in the same area.

Looking for topaz in Texas is more work than the casual rock hunter may want to attempt. The terrain is rugged and you will need a shovel, pick and a wooden framed screen for sifting dirt.

Topaz, an aluminum fluorosilicate, is heavier than the surrounding sand and dirt and will sink into mud when it rains. Therefore, many of the finds are made in stream beds. It may be necessary to dig down six to eight feet, then shovel and sift dirt in hopes of finding the prized topaz. Another common place for finds is along the stream banks. At one point a rainstorm washed out the banks and left an overburden, allowing many topaz nuggets to be found.

Having found a topaz, it can then be cut for gem purposes. It is one of the few stones in Texas that is cut for gem use. A word of caution: you will find that the cost of cutting is high and it should only be done if you plan to keep the stone as a collector's item.

TOURMALINE

A complex silicate of boron and aluminum, *tourmaline* often contains other elements that create different colors. The types that occur in Texas are black (*schorl*) and brown (*dravite*) and have a glassy luster. Tourmaline is hard and cannot be scratched with a steel file.

Some varieties of this material are used extensively as gemstones, but most of what is found in Texas is not of significant gem quality.

The dark brown and black material found in Llano County is usually mixed with quartz and is very nearly opaque. In fact, it looks a great deal like coal. Occasionally, it shows a hexagonal crystal habit with well formed terminals.

Although tourmaline is sometimes used as an abrasive by industry, there is none produced in Texas for that purpose.

CENTRAL TEXAS COLLECTION SITES

LLANO

From Austin, take State Highway 290 west, then go northwest on State Highway 71. About 14 miles southeast of Llano by the side of the road is a historical marker and two huge boulders of solid white and pink *(rose)* quartz. (Please look, but don't touch.)

Continue on to Llano and from there, go 9.4 miles north on State Highway 16 to a roadside park.

At the park there is a step-over so that you have easy access to the outcroppings. There you will find exposed hills of rock.

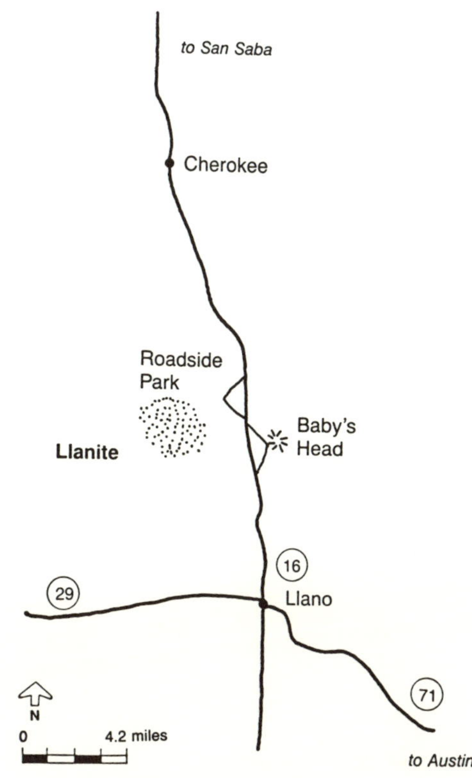

Llanite outcropping.

The pink llanite is heavily streaked with veins of milky quartz. Occasionally, there are large pockets of quartz material.

Look for a finely grained pinkish-orange material with small dark specks about the size of a pinhead. It is relatively easy to break off a piece with the pick. The quartz veins are milky and translucent, and extremely hard, so be sure to wear eye protection.

Across the road from the roadside park, there is a circular dirt road that provides a view of what is known as Baby Head, a hill of llanite. This area is fenced, so confine collecting to the roadside park area.

SAN SABA

Travel 2.2 miles west from the town of San Saba on State Highway 190, then turn left on farm road 1030 and follow that for 6.9 miles. Turn left again at the house and large red barn,

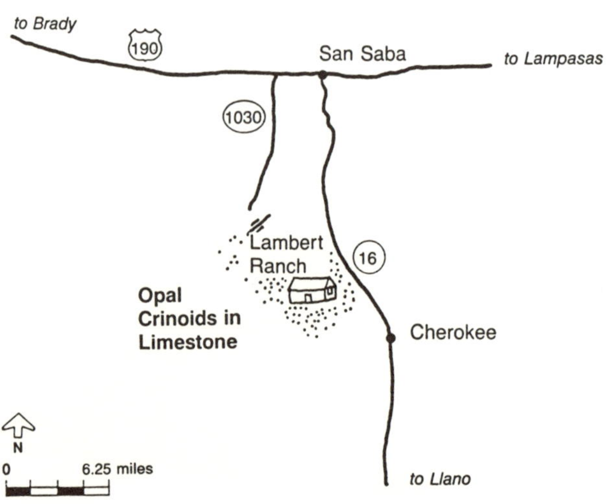

Crinoid-bearing limestone.

cross a cattle guard and continue about 2 miles to the ranch house of C. B. Lambert. Mr. Lambert welcomes collectors and will act as your guide for a very reasonable fee. It is necessary for him to accompany you since there are no roads to the collecting areas. He is very knowledgeable and has many stories to share with rockhunters.

We found opalized coral, common opal, small crystalline calcite specimens and crinoids in white limestone. The coral will be black in contrast to the white limestone, with a radiating circular shape. The opal has the appearance of a thin white translucent coating on the limestone. The crinoid stem is mostly what is found in the limestone. It has the appearance of cylindrical ribbed tubing, not unlike the look of electrical conduit. A prized find is a cross section of the stem that exhibits a five-pointed star pattern.

Crinoids also appear in pink and dark gray limestone here, but be warned that this is harder than white limestone so be careful when using your prospector's hammer. The hardness does allow it to take a good polish and it is often cut into spheres, for paperweights or desk sets.

Polished pink limestone with crinoids.

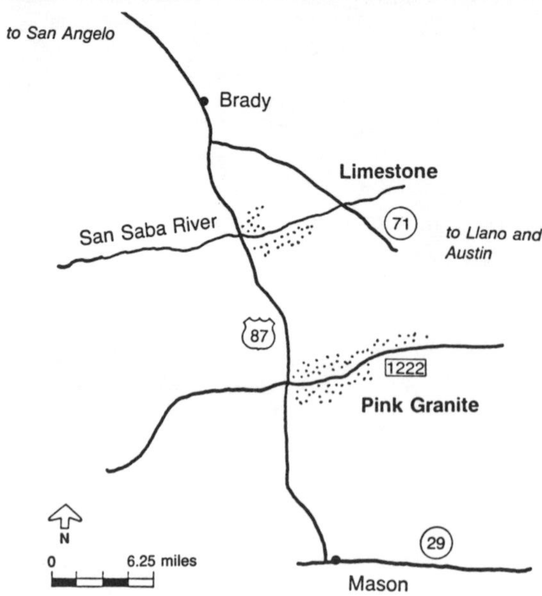

KATEMCY CREEK AREA

Go south from the town of Brady on State Highway 87. Near the San Saba River bridge, you will spot limestone formations that contain crinoids. Further south, turn left on FM 1222 and go about a mile and a half. This area abounds with outcroppings of pink granite. The slow cooling of the magma produced granite with feldspar crystals that are easily distinguishable. Much of the material is on private property, but there are plenty of the rounded rocks available on the side of the road. We collected some fine samples containing large feldspar crystals mixed with quartz and pyrite. This was the best and most accessible area we found for collecting the large grained pink granite.

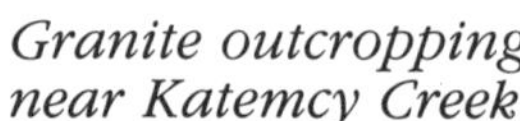
Granite outcropping near Katemcy Creek.

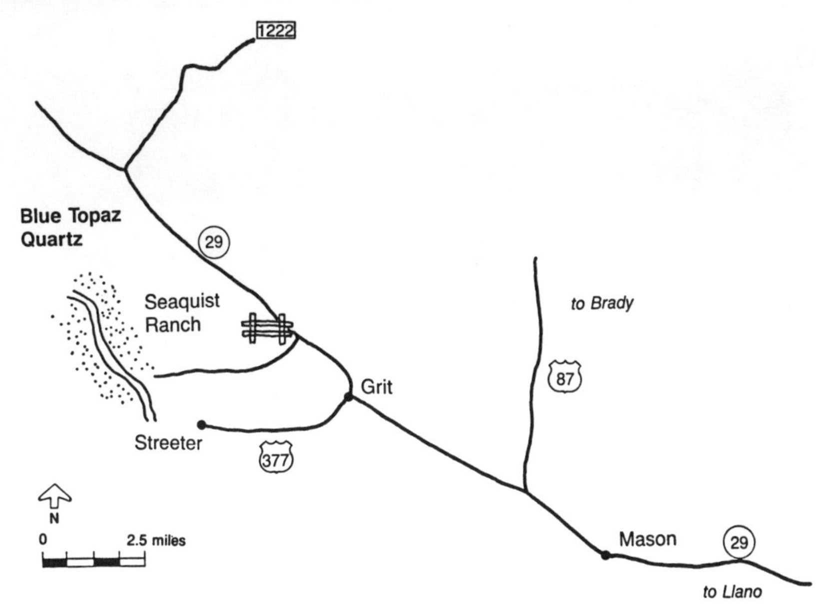

MASON COUNTY

From the town of Brady continue south on Highway 87 until it intersects Highway 29 at a roadside park. Bear right on 29 to Grit and you will come to a house and an abandoned store. Mrs. Wesley Loeffler has keys to two sites for topaz hunters: the Seaquist and Hoffman ranches. She will collect the fee and give you directions to either or both.

Topaz and smoky quartz territory in Texas is generally on private property. The Seaquist Ranch is perhaps the most famous place to hunt for the stone. There is a per day, per person charge and you must obtain a key.

After getting your key, drive to the gate. There is a designated parking area for cars and camping vehicles. Proceed from there to the stream beds and start digging.

We visited this location twice, once in May and once in October, but never found a topaz. To find one, it is imperative that all conditions be right: it must have rained hard within the past few weeks, the stream should be dry for easy access and the overburden not be too great for a person with a shovel to handle. It is seldom that all the conditions are right.

Some guidelines while looking for topaz and smoky quartz: the crystals will seldom be in a shape that is immediately recognizable. Most often the topaz and smoky quartz will be in pebbles about the size of a quarter. Through a process of weathering and tumbling with other rocks in the stream, the surface will have dulled to a frosty coating. Topaz can sometimes be recognized by its cleavage if there is a fine sheer break at any point on the crystal. The quartz may exhibit a vitreous (glassy) fracture. The colorless topaz is generally more common than the pale blue, but you never know till you look. Quartz will range from colorless to deep smoky brown.

If you should find such a stone, don't break it for identification purposes. Instead, take it to someone who can tell you

Stream bed—Seaquist Ranch.

what you have found. Gem and mineral club members will be helpful there.

Although when we visited the Seaquist ranch, the area hadn't had any significant rain in over two years, it is both authors' opinion that the Seaquist Ranch experience (at $20.00 for the both of us) was not worth the money. It takes more than persistence to find a topaz; it takes a rugged constitution, the proper equipment, and a tenacious spirit. If you have only a few hours to look for a topaz, perhaps this stop is better left till you can spend a weekend at it.

The Hoffman ranch adjoins the Seaquist, but the terrain is rugged and requires a four-wheel drive vehicle to get to the topaz-bearing ground. Lack of rain has affected prospects here as well. There has been so little rain that all other private ranches where topaz can be found have been closed to rockhunters because of fire danger.

POINTS OF INTEREST

FREDERICKSBURG

This charming town settled by German immigrants in 1846 still retains its old world flavor. It has numerous interesting shops and quaint bed and breakfast rooms if you want to spend the night. The Admiral Nimitz Center is worth a visit as is the Lady Bird Johnson State Park.

ENCHANTED ROCK

This state park is located 18 miles north of Fredericksburg on FM 965. There is an admission fee to get into the park.

Enchanted Rock is a large granite batholith that, over many centuries, has worked its way to the surface. Molten rock or magma intruded through older rocks and then cooled slowly causing the formation of large feldspar crystals in this granite. This bald dome is rounded because of the process called "spal-

Enchanted Rock, while off limits for rock collecting, offers the place in Texas to see an intrusive igneous rock formation.

ling'' whereby concentric layers of rock peel back due to contraction and expansions with temperature changes.

This square mile of rock was once sacred to the Indians who fought to keep the white man away. Today, it has been designated a state park and collecting rock is forbidden. However, there is no better place in the state to observe the formation of intrusive igneous rock and it is a must for any rock lover.

INNER SPACE CAVERNS

On I-35 north of Austin, near Georgetown, this cavern features impressive displays of stalactites, stalagmites and flowstone in addition to remains of Ice Age animals. Don't miss the ''cave bacon.'' There is an admission charge.

LONGHORN CAVERNS STATE PARK

Located on Highway 281 about 11 miles southwest of Burnet on Park Road 4 is the world's third largest cavern and boasts two miles of underground paths.

Section 2

WEST TEXAS

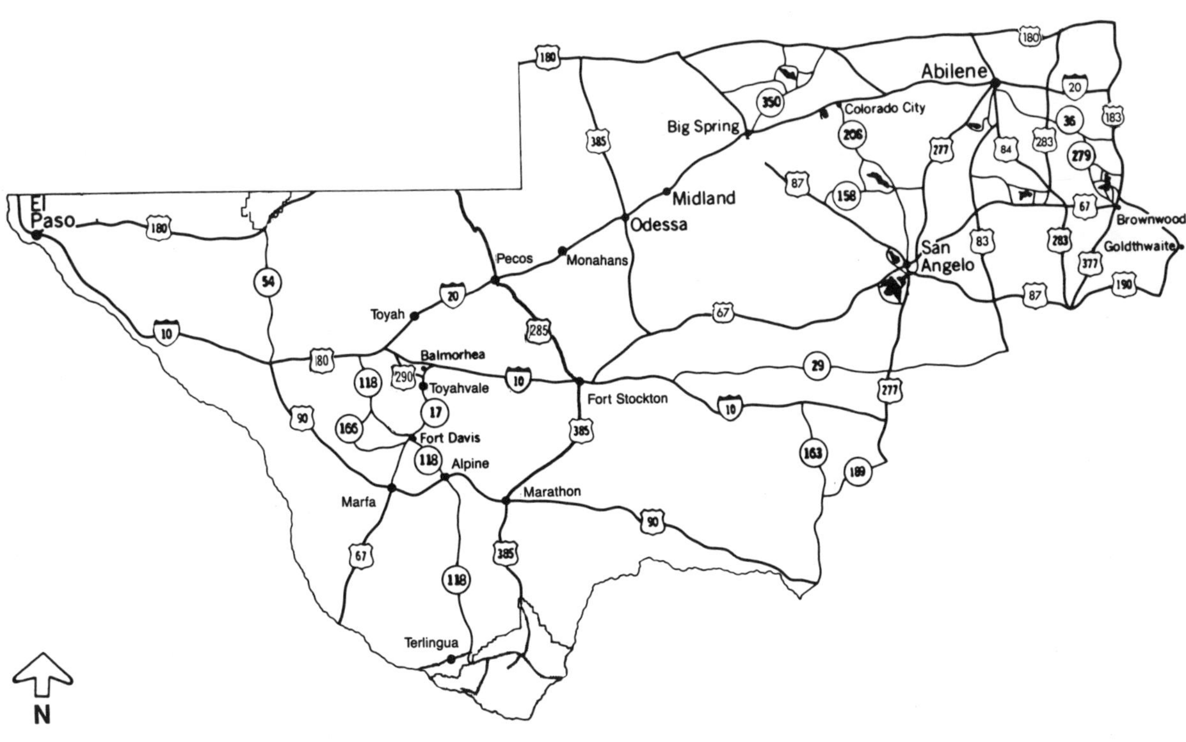

INTRODUCTION

This area of the far west portion of the state is geologically known as the Trans Pecos. It is bordered by the Rio Grande River on the south, El Paso on the west, and Midland-Odessa at the northeast and includes Big Bend National Park. Much of the interesting landscape dates from the Tertiary period some forty million years ago.

From the edge of the flat high plains at Midland-Odessa you drive west across dry desert, completely unforested and exposed to the elements, into the rugged volcanic Davis Mountains. Their starkness holds a certain kind of beauty; nature's work revealed. Vegetation is sparse, and the volcanic formation of mountains is still visible on the surface, as if formed only yesterday. The flow of molten rock is easy to detect when perusing the landscape or examining individual rock.

Farther on, past the bluffs and peaks dotting the barren terrain and into Big Bend National Park, are the spectacular Chisos Mountains. Viewing them from the Chisos Mountain Basin, a ring of volcanic formation has developed cool mountain vegetation, unlike any other part of Texas. The 5,400 foot elevation makes the temperature a pleasant contrast to the surrounding desert-like climate.

The spectacular mountains of west Texas are volcanic or extrusive igneous rocks with some of the area being intrusive, having forced its way through sedimentary type ground.

That fact is obvious when one views them jutting abruptly out of the flat landscape.

Being volcanic in nature, this area is abundant with wonderful rockhunting. Most of the rocks are concentrated into several general groups.

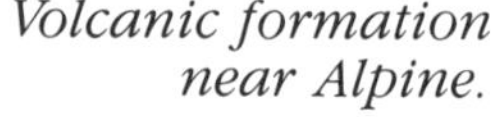

Volcanic formation near Alpine.

AGATE

A term given to semi-transparent and translucent chalcedony is *agate*. It takes many forms and shapes and is found extensively in this part of the state. The famous red and black plume agate comes from around Alpine. The plumes are created by the tree-like dendritic formation that creates unusual designs in the agate. When the agate forms in delicate bands of differing colors, it's called crazy lace agate and can occur in varying pastels of blue, white, gray, lavender and colorless. Pom-pom agate is another interesting find from this area. The pom is created by the clustered formation of dendritic material into a rounded shape. All of these can be cut and polished and are sometimes used in jewelry.

A solid light blue agate that sometimes exhibits a black plume, is found around Lake Balmorhea. It is a very translucent, dense material and takes a high polish.

A very hard, compact, semi-translucent (nearly opaque) variety of chalcedony is called *jasper*. It occurs most often as red,

Crazy lace agate.

Black plume agate.

brown or yellow, often banded with several of those colors in the same stone. Weathered pieces can be recognized if they have been chipped by the conchoidal fracture. Again, as with all agates, this material takes a good polish.

Black plume agate.

CALCITE

Our old friend, the calcium carbonate, is found as a transparent or translucent, colorless, white or brownish mineral sometimes mixed with other substances. It can be recognized by its distinct cleavage or by fizzing when in contact with a drop of dilute solution of hydrochloric acid. It can also be scratched with a copper penny since it is soft. Calcite is a very common mineral and can be found in several different formations occurring in this part of the state. *Dog-tooth spar* is a pointed crystal formation that is found in geodes (see glossary for geodes).

CINNABAR

The mercuric sulfide or mercury ore called cinnabar was mined in west Texas beginning about 1894. It was found in the Terlingua area of Brewster County, but the mines are now closed and not safe for exploring. Cinnabar occurs as dark red or yellow-red in color and is often mixed with other substances such as clay, calcite or iron oxide.

We purchased a small piece of cinnabar at a small rock shop on Highway 118 just north of the entrance to Big Bend National Park. It's worth the stop just to talk to the elderly German lady who owns the shop.

Tours are directed at the Villa de la Mina three miles west of Terlingua on Highway 170. Collectors are allowed to examine the trailings (mining refuse) that cover thousands of acres surrounding the mine. Look for a reddish-brown streak in the rocks found there.

FLUORITE

Calcium fluoride is transparent to translucent, colorless or white with a glassy luster. Other minerals present cause such colors as pink, green, purple, brown or blue.

Fluorite is soft enough to be scratched with a pocket knife and leaves a white streak. It is easily recognized by its four directions of cleavage. Carefully broken, the material can be separated to create an octohedron shape (a pyramid, base to base).

The largest deposits of the material in Texas are in the Eagle Mountains of Hudspeth County where it has risen to the surface through cracks in igneous rock. Fluorite can be found here in commercial quantities as it has a great many industrial uses: steel making, glass making and manufacture of hydrofluoric acid.

GALENA

Lead sulfide, which is a very heavy, shiny, metallic substance is called galena. It is so soft that it will mark paper leaving a gray-black streak. It also has three directions of perfect cleavage that sometimes leave cube shaped fragments.

Galena formed when magma forced out solutions that contained lead as it moved through cracks of rocks depositing on their surfaces.

In West Texas, galena was once closely associated with the mining of silver, but is now found to be an important source of lead.

HEMATITE

The chief ore of iron, iron oxide, is hematite. Its occurrence is scattered around the state, but nowhere is it found in abundance. It has a metallic luster and the color range is reddish brown, dark brown, gray or black. The soft, red earth-like material is called "red ocher."

Texas hematite occurs as rounded masses or granular clumps in Hudspeth County of far West Texas.

When fine, steely gray masses are found, it is sometimes cut for gemstone purposes as it is in men's jewelry.

MICA

Mica is the name given to a group of similar minerals that have one perfect direction of cleavage that is parallel to the base of the crystal. This is called basal cleavage and allows the mineral to be separated into thin sheets called "books."

Two mica minerals that are found in Texas are *muscovite* and *biotite,* both potassium-aluminum silicates. Colors include light brown, yellow, green, dark green, brown and black. They are extremely soft and can be scratched with a copper penny.

Mica is very heat resistant and has been used as insulating material and for the manufacture of such diverse things as tubes for industry to Christmas tree "snow."

Not much of the material is found in Texas, but a fair grade of sheet mica is found in the Mica Mine in West Texas.

OBSIDIAN

A volcanically formed glass that occurs naturally as an igneous rock is called *obsidian.* It contains feldspar and quartz, just as granite does, but forms when the lava cools and hardens before the minerals have time to crystallize.

It is smooth and shiny, usually dark green or dark brown and semi-translucent, allowing light to pass through. The curved shape of a broken edge is called conchoidal fracture and is very sharp. This sharp edge allowed the west Texas Indians to carve the material into arrowheads that were quite efficient.

Rounded, tumbled pieces of obsidian that are a dark smoky color and transparent or translucent are called "Apache tears" and can be found in Brewster and Presidio Counties.

OPAL

Precious opal, or that with a play of color has been found in the Alpine area of Brewster County. This translucent material might have flashes of orange, red, blue and green. (See section 1 for a complete description.)

However, common opal is more often found filling the cracks of volcanic material in this part of the state. Its appearance is that of a thin white translucent vein contained within other rocks.

QUARTZ

As discussed before, quartz is a very common material, silicon dioxide, but it takes many forms. Crystalline quartz exhibits large distinct crystals with easily recognizable hexagonal shapes. Sometimes quartz forms in massive groups of small crystals that often cover the surface of another material. This often gives the appearance of a "frosting" of quartz on the other substance.

Cryptocrystalline quartz occurs as a mass, where the individual crystals are much too small to be seen with the naked eye or even with the average microscope. They exhibit no evidence of hexagonal shape. Instead, the material appears as a hard, dense,

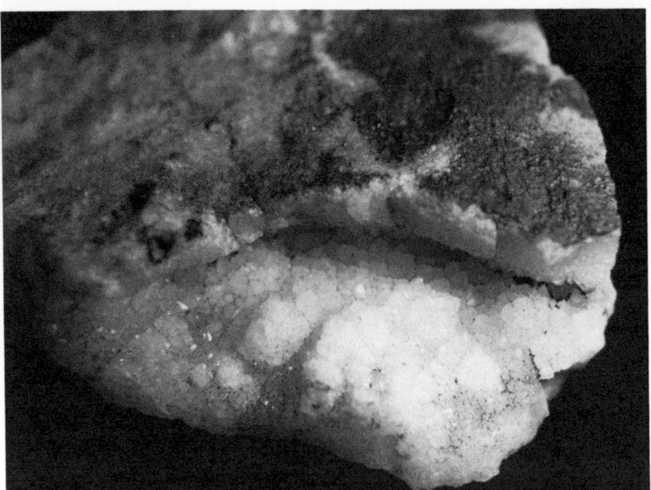

Massive quartz.

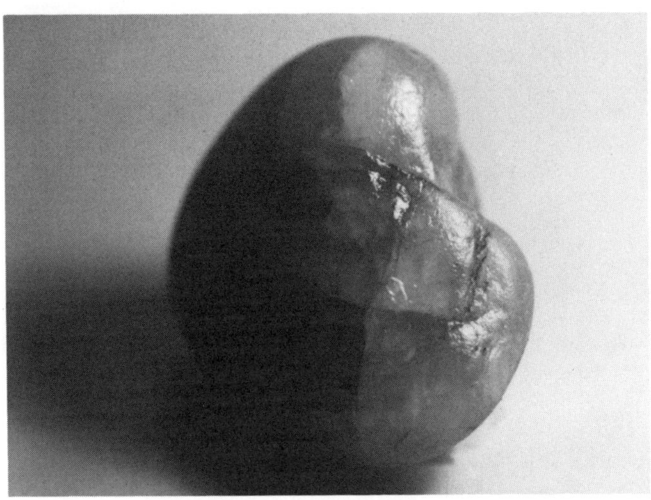

Weathered quartz rock.

even, smooth mass. This is called *chalcedony* (pronounced kal-SED-on-e).

In this area of the state, quartz has been found in all of these forms. Probably the most prized of all quartz finds is the amethyst geode. Geodes are rounded hollow masses that occur with limestone, when the crystals form from the outside to the inside as mineral laden water seeps into the limestone cavity. The outer surface is dull and uninteresting, but when broken open reveals crystals radiating toward the center. If they are a lovely purple quartz, it is amethyst, but they also occur with colorless or milky white crystals.

Many quartz finds are a distortion of the geode. Maybe, in the process of formation, the geode was broken open and it could not form in the normal way. Or sometimes, the cavity of a geode is completely filled with crystalline mass. In other words, it is very common to find quartz geodes in other than perfect formation.

SANDSTONE

As the name implies, *sandstone* is made up of grains of sand that have broken off and weathered from rocks and minerals. When grains of sand become cemented together it is called sandstone. The cement is made up of minerals that have dissolved in water and washed over the sand grains, and as it deposits itself on the grains, acts as a cement binding the grains together.

Sandstone is found in many colors, depending upon which minerals have been dissolved in the cementing solution. It can be pale cream, tan, red, brown, green or dark gray. Often it occurs in bands of varying colors. It can even occur with dendrite inclusions. Dendritic formation is that which has the look of tree branching and is often seen on rocks of many types.

Dendritic formation on green sandstone.

SELENITE

Selenite is a colorless, glassy and transparent variety of gypsum. It is found in clusters or as flat and prism-shaped crystals. Sometimes these crystals twin to each other forming a chevron pattern.

The material can be recognized by the cleavage property. Selenite has four directions of cleavage, one so perfect that some of it splits into thin sheets that have a similar appearance to mica, but unlike mica, the material is brittle and will break if bent.

If selenite is confused with any material, it is calcite, but the two can be distinguished by placing a few drops of dilute hydrochloric acid on the rock. The calcite will bubble and fizz, but selenite will not.

When the material forms in cluster groupings it takes on a floral motif called "rosettes" and often has a pinkish-orange color. These are highly prized by collectors.

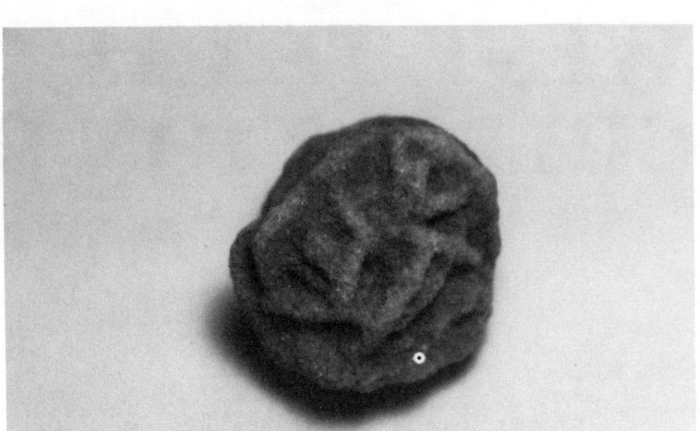
Selenite rose.

The material makes most attractive specimens, but its softness makes it impractical for cutting and polishing for gem use.

SILVER

Silver is a shiny white metal that has long been considered, along with gold and platinum, a precious metal. And also, like them, it is an element as well as a mineral.

When found alone it is called native silver and easy to recognize. It has a metallic luster that is silver white in color that may tarnish to a gray or black. It is heavy and soft, scratching with a pocket knife. When it occurs as crystals, it can take three shapes: reticulate (net-like), acicular (needles), and filiform (wires).

Texas silver-bearing minerals, argentite and cerargyrite, do not resemble silver at all. Argentite is silver sulfide and a dark lead-gray color that weathers to a dull black. Cerargyrite is a silver chloride.

There are several famous mines in Texas that are no longer in production. The Presidio Mine near Shafter in south central Presidio County operated between 1885 and 1942. The Hazel Mine is now idle and flooded. There is no silver currently being mined in the state.

TALC

A hydrous magnesium silicate that is extremely soft is known as *talc*. It is 1 on the hardness scale and can be scratched with the fingernail. It is also tectile, meaning that it can be cut through with a knife.

When it forms into a stone, it has a distinctly greasy or soapy feel, and is consequently named "soapstone." The color is white, light green or gray and leaves a white streak.

Usual formation is massive, or in large fist-shape bunches instead of crystals. It is found as a metamorphic rock in Hudspeth County just north of Highway 80 near Allamoore. These are open pit mines and not ideal collecting sites.

WEST TEXAS COLLECTION SITES

TOYAH

Nineteen miles west of Pecos on Interstate 20 (Highway 80) is the small town of Toyah. On a ranch road southeast of town we found an abundance of samples right along the roadside. We picked up common opal on banded volcanic rock, banded sandstone and dark red jasper.

The opal has the appearance of a white, milky translucent rock coating. The sandstone was red, yellow, green or banded with several colors, some dendritic. The jasper was small, about the size of a half dollar, even, dense and hard.

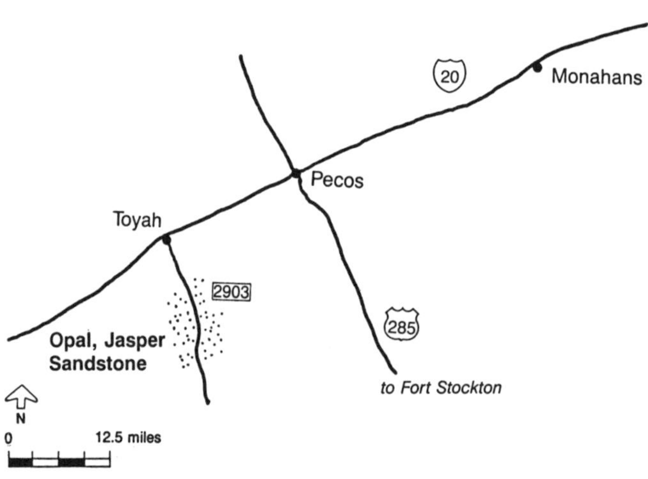

LAKE BALMORHEA

The town of Balmorhea is located near the intersection of State Highway 17 and Interstate 10 approximately 50 miles west of Fort Stockton. It is a very small town and on Houston

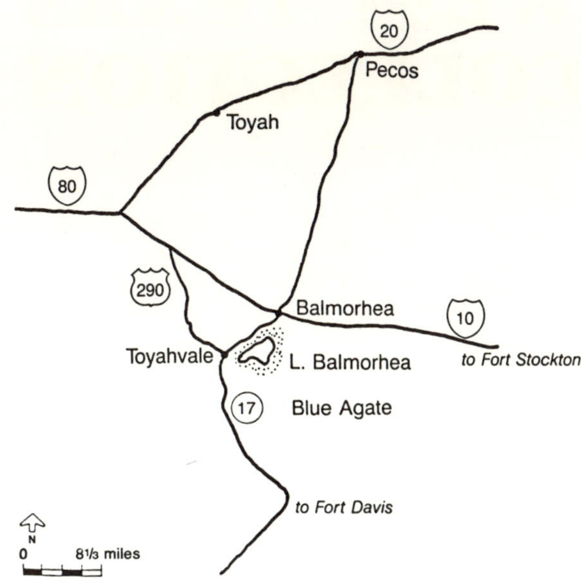

Street there is a sign which directs you to "Fishing Lake." Watch carefully for the sign; it is easy to miss.

We hunted the south shores of the lake, and while there were many rocks, the well-known Balmorhea Blue Agate wasn't very plentiful. We searched a long time before finding a few samples of this. Out best sample was a large flat rock about five inches in diameter. The surface was pitted but under closer observation and with a helpful blow of the hammer, we discovered that it was, indeed, the famous Balmorhea Blue Agate. We also found a handful of red-banded agate rocks.

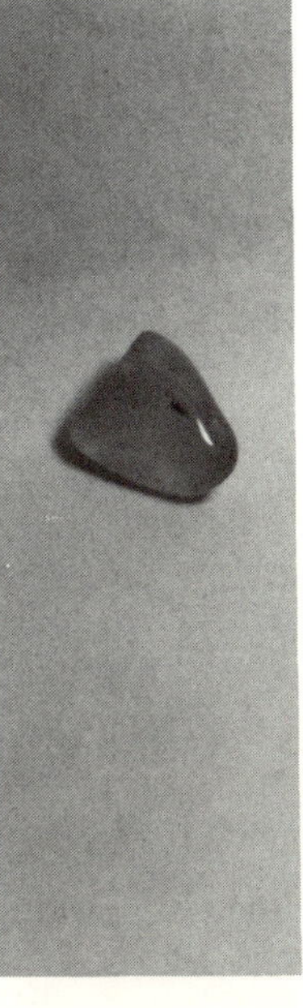

Left photo: Balmorhea blue agate.

Right photo: Tumbled Balmorhea blue agate.

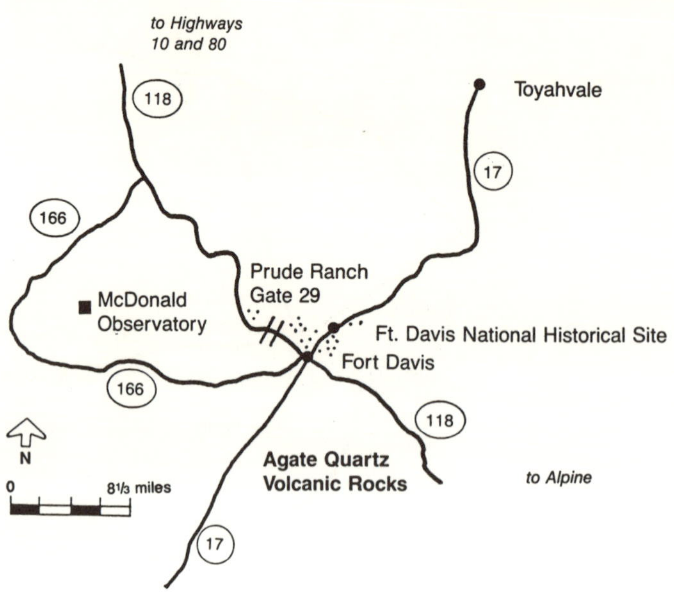

FORT DAVIS

This historic and scenic West Texas town is located some 50 miles south of Balmorhea on Highway 17. Take Highway 118 north past the McDonald Observatory turnoff. Easily observable rock formations are of interest and just off the side of the road, we collected dark red jasper with calcite crystals in it.

On Highway 118 about five miles northwest of Fort Davis, near the Prude Ranch Gate 29, we found quartz, jasper and banded sandstone by the roadside. There are abundant samples near the highway; it is not necessary to go onto private property to collect.

We found evidence of geode formation, but mostly broken pieces, and igneous rocks with quartz crystal formations on top of them. We also found lots of multi-color sandstone.

Left photo: Dark red jasper with calcite.

Right photo: Quartz from Prude Ranch—Gate 29 area.

Drusey quartz—Prude Ranch, Gate 29 area.

Closer to McDonald Observatory on 118, we found small calcite crystals in sedimentary rock and light olive green chalcedony.

Just outside Fort Davis State Park on 118, there is a drainage wash that runs under the highway bridge. Quartz crystals abound here and the dedicated hunter can also find geodes.

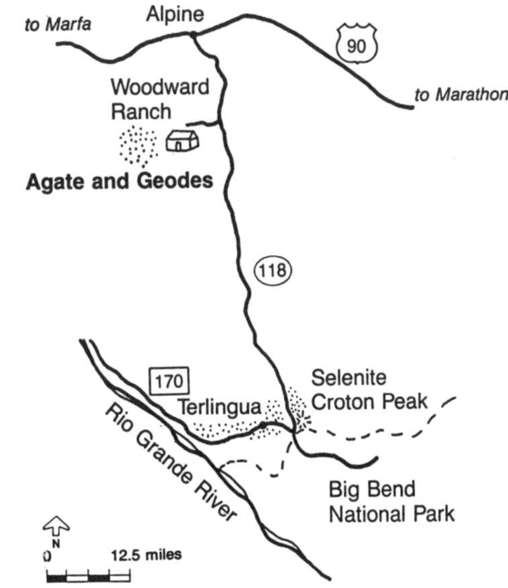

WOODWARD RANCH

Sixteen miles south of Alpine on Highway 118, a sign directs you onto a dirt road to the ranch. About two miles west, you will find one of the state's most well-known and productive rockhunting sites. A family member is usually on hand to greet and point you in the right direction. Agate is plentiful and we gathered some fine examples of plume and crazy lace. The

Agate geode from Woodward Ranch.

Crazy lace agate from Woodward Ranch.

Woodwards charge a price per pound for the rough, uncut material. For a reasonable fee, they will also cut it for you. In the event that you don't have time to do any hunting, they have abundant rough material for sale, as well as a large selection of cut and polished goods.

Many of the igneous rocks found here have a very porous look to them, and one can almost see how they formed. It isn't hard to imagine them as magma being thrown from the earth's surface to be cooled quickly by the air. These are often agate, but not suitable for cutting because the material is not dense.

You'll find this a most satisfying trip and will have to limit what to take with you because of weight.

Farther south, the Woodwards have another ranch in the Needle Peak area. Here you will find the unusual pom pom and thistle agates. You need to make arrangements at the Alpine ranch and Mr. Woodward will act as your guide. The trip requires most of a day and must be made in an all-terrain vehicle, so there is a fee for Mr. Woodward's services.

CROTON PEAK

Approximately 100 miles south of Alpine on 118, just north of the intersection with Highway 170, is Croton Peak. The sandy hills extend to the edge of the highway and glistening displays of selenite are readily visible from your car. You need only stop along the roadside to find many good examples.

The colorless to white crystals sparkle in the sunlight and are easy to see. The small flat crystals are very fragile, so there is no need to use a hammer on them. Handle carefully.

At Croton Peak you can find many good examples of selenite along the roadside.

TERLINGUA

At the intersection of Highways 118-170, go west on 170 to the famous ghost town of Terlingua. Amid the sagebrush and sandy soil on Solitario Saw Mill Road, we gathered more selenite, as well as basalt. The selenite here was white and tended to form in clumps of crystals at angles to each other, much like a large version of a selenite rose. The basalt is very dark brown or black and opaque, with its igneous formation obvious from the pitted surface.

If you want to hunt for cinnabar, ask at the local store for the best location. Be sure to be dressed properly and have water with you as this area can be very hot in the summer.

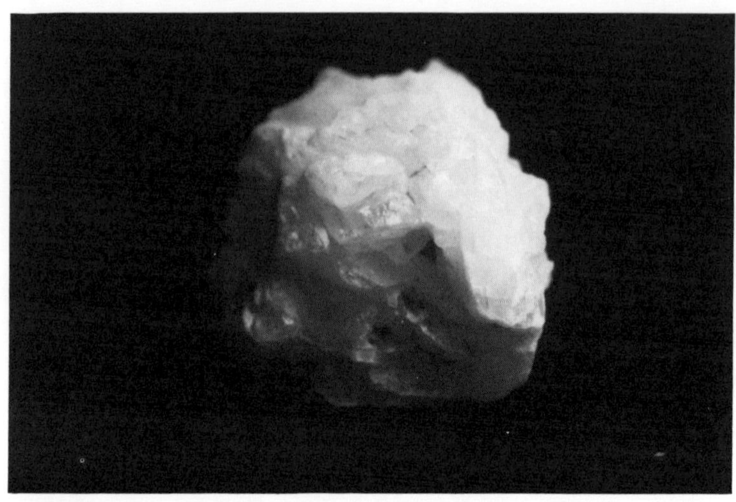

Selenite from Terlingua area tends to be white and forms in clumps of crystals.

Basalt from Terlingua area.

POINTS OF INTEREST

MCDONALD OBSERVATORY

Sixteen miles northwest of Fort Davis via Highway 118, atop 6,791 ft Mount Locke, the University of Texas operates one of the nation's largest reflector telescopes. A visitor center at the foot of the peak presents an informative program throughout the day and the telescope can be viewed from the visitor's gallery. Special arrangements can be made to look through it by writing in advance.

FORT DAVIS

This National Historic Site is located inside the town of Fort Davis and provides visitors a unique look at life on a frontier outpost as it was over a century ago. There is an admission fee.

BIG BEND

This national park covers over 700,000 acres and provides spectacular examples of varied terrain. The awesome canyons of the Rio Grande, jungle-type flood plain, Chihuahuan Desert and cool elevations of the Chisos Mountains treat visitors to as much diverse scenery as can be found anywhere.

SUL ROSS UNIVERSITY-UNIVERSITY OF THE BIG BEND

Located on the Alpine campus, this museum features Indian artifacts and other items of frontier life.

TERLINGUA

The once-thriving town revolved around mercury mining before the boom ended. Its claim to fame is now the annual World Championship Chili Cook-Off which is attended by thousands every fall.

MONAHANS SANDHILLS

This state park is located just off Interstate 20 about 50 miles west of Odessa. Unusual wind-sculptured sand dunes create a Sahara-like landscape that covers over 4,000 acres. There is a modern museum and interpretative center with an admission charge.

Section 3

NORTH TEXAS

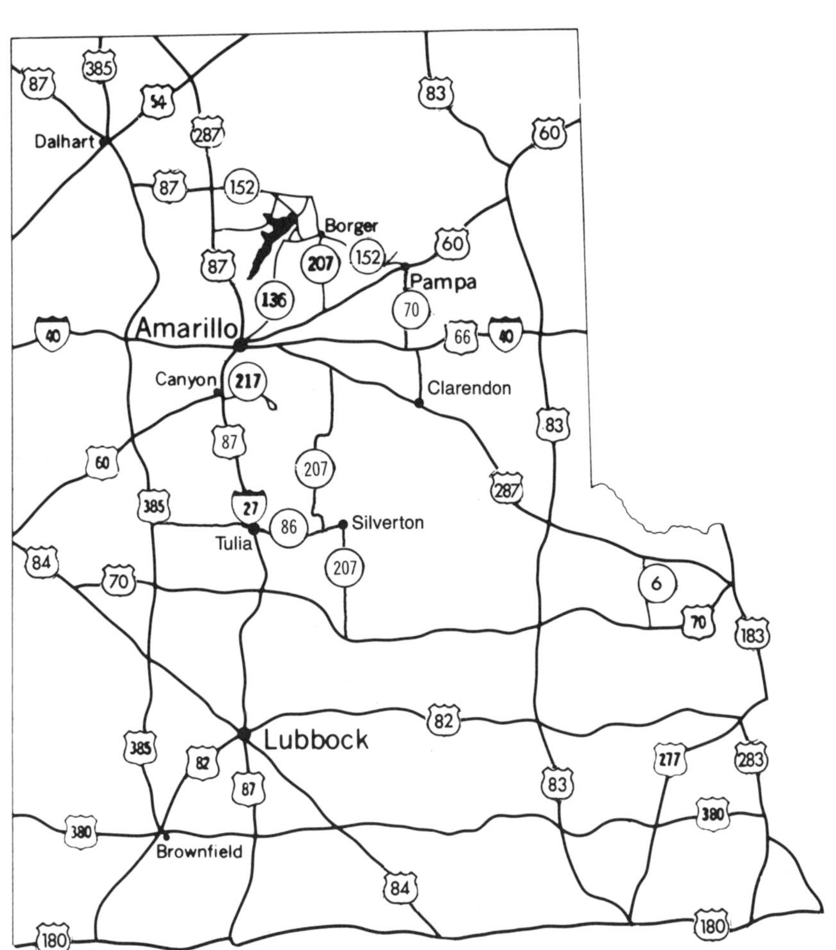

INTRODUCTION

North Texas is generally known as the plains region, be it the high plains of the Panhandle or the central plains that follow the Red River eastward to the lightly rolling hills of the East Texas grand prairie.

The high plains, with an elevation of 3500 feet and surface slope of only eight feet per mile, is most aptly named. It is a sheet of sand and clay that was deposited less than ten million years ago. Wind and water leveled any existing differences in topography. Where rivers have cut into this vast monotonous expanse and carried away the layers, we are able to observe the geology of the land.

There is evidence that the pushing-up of this great flat expanse in sporadic bursts is still taking place. This constant movement causes a slipping along any existing fault line (i.e., earthquake).

This area is bordered by the state's boundary on the west and north, the central mineral region in the south and Highway 183 in the east.

DOLOMITE

Dolomite is the name for both a mineral, calcium-magnesium carbonate, and a rock. It has a glassy or pearly luster and occurs in such colors as white, pink, brown or gray. It leaves a white streak and is soft enough to be scratched with a pocket knife.

Texas dolomite is found in coarse, medium and fine-grained masses making up dolomite rock. In some cases, it can resemble

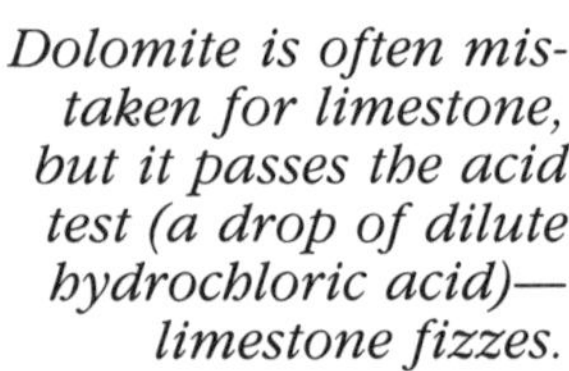

Dolomite is often mistaken for limestone, but it passes the acid test (a drop of dilute hydrochloric acid)—limestone fizzes.

limestone, but can be easily distinguished with a drop of dilute hydrochloric acid. The limestone will fizz.

The appearance is that of a finely-grained sugar cube. This has often been cut and polished as an ornamental stone for spheres and desk sets.

Commercial uses include road building materials and flooring.

FLINT

Flint is the smooth, even, massive form of the cryptocrystalline quartz, chalcedony. Found in this part of Texas it is called *novaculite*, and has a cream base color with swirling bands of tan running throughout it. It strongly resembles Alibates Flint. It is most readily seen among rocks and boulders in stream beds of the high plains. It has been found around Lake McClellan.

Novaculite is a type of flint that has a cream base color and swirling bands of tan running through it.

FOSSILS

Various fossils are found in this section of the state, most notably near Cisco in Eastland County of the central plains area. Here, the topsoil is being constantly eroded, and upper and lower Cretaceous fossils are revealed.

Crinoid stems, coral, brachiopods, pelecypods and trilobites have been found in the road cuts of state Highway 6 between Cisco and Moran.

GNEISS

Pronounced "nice," this is a metamorphic rock that forms in parallel light and dark bands. It must possess these bands in order to be gneiss and can be formed either as an igneous rock or as a sedimentary rock where the earth's heat, fluids and pressures caused the metamorphosis.

Most gneiss has the same components as granite (quartz and feldspar) and is of the same hardness. Some central Texas gneiss is made up of sandstone and is pink in color. Another type is altered igneous rock and gray in color.

JASPER

Being the abundant chalcedony material that it is, jasper is found in this part of the state as well as the others. In every stream bed there are pebbles of multi-color jasper: red, yellow, orange. Most of it is small, having been weathered for many hundreds of years and not suitable for cutting purposes, but these little rocks are wonderful for the rockhound who has a tumbler.

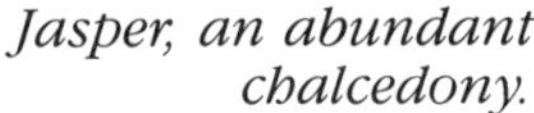

Jasper, an abundant chalcedony.

PETRIFIED WOOD AND PALM

Wood or *palmwood*, when petrified, is no longer wood. It is now agate, a quartz material (see Section 4 for complete description). For this reason it is heavy and dense, but will still have the pattern of the original wood. It has been found in the Lake MacKenzie area of the Panhandle.

PITCHBLENDE

Pitchblende is a dark colored uranium mineral that is a variety of uranium dioxide. It has no crystal shape, but occurs in rounded masses that are black, greenish black and brownish black. It is heavy and so hard that it can only be scratched with a steel file. The luster is sub-metallic and dull with a brownish black streak.

The material is radioactive, but the uranium occurs only in combination with other minerals and not alone. When a uranium mineral is found (there are at least five), it can be detected with a Geiger counter. For the entire life of the mineral, the uranium is in the process of breaking down into other elements. It is therefore radioactive.

These minerals are not plentiful enough in Texas to be mined, but do occur as dark greenish black massive formations, usually heavily weathered.

SELENITE

A colorless, glassy transparent variety of gypsum is *selenite*. (See Section 2, West Texas for full description.)

This part of the state produces fine specimens of the material that occur in crystals as long as one foot. The gypsum has a ten-

Transparent selenite sliver.

Transparent selenite.

dency to pick up coloration from surrounding minerals. That found in an area with dark red sandy soil will be a dark red-brown color.

The bright shiny surfaces and perfect cleavage make it very easy to recognize. The lack of large individual crystals makes it unreasonable to cut, however, and is best left as a specimen find.

Clump of selenite crystals—Lake Mackenzie.

NORTH TEXAS COLLECTION SITES

LAKE MACKENZIE

Travel south from Amarillo on Interstate 27 to Tulia (approximately 75 miles). Go east on Highway 86 and north on 207 about 20 miles to reach the lake entrance. Cross the dam and stop at the office and store to get your permit and a map. Just after you cross the dam, there is a hill sparkling with selenite crystals. There is plenty of material still in formation as well as broken crystals. Thin pieces of the material are colorless, but in formation, they are a light green color. We found some crystals as long as one foot. The lucky hunter will find a selenite rose. The hunting here is excellent.

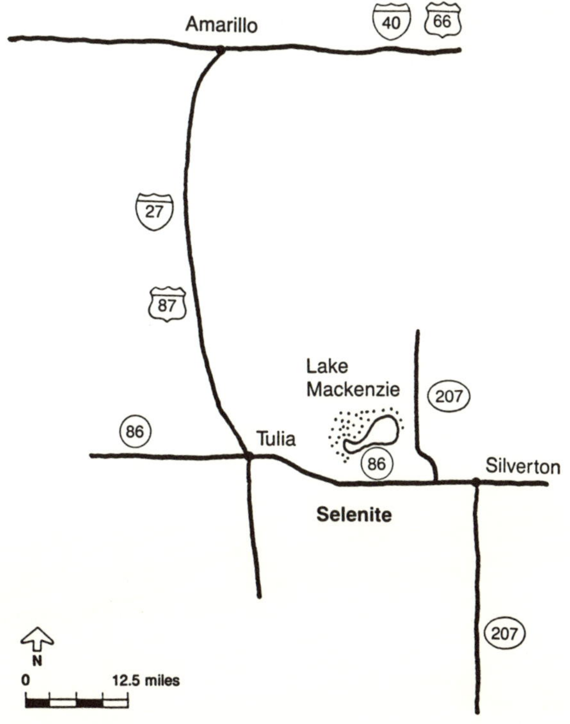

Lake Mackenzie.

Follow the lake road around to the north side of the lake and you will find more selenite. Here the samples are embedded in red sandy hills and have taken on the color of their surroundings. These are unusual and interesting.

GREEN BELT RESERVOIR

About 60 miles east of Amarillo, Interstate 40 intersects with Highway 70. Follow 70 south to the lake entrance and pick up a permit from the lake office. Just north of the bridge over the Salt Fork of the Red River, turn onto the dirt road which winds along the base of the cliffs.

Here, quartz occurs in massive formation rather than crystals as large rocks.

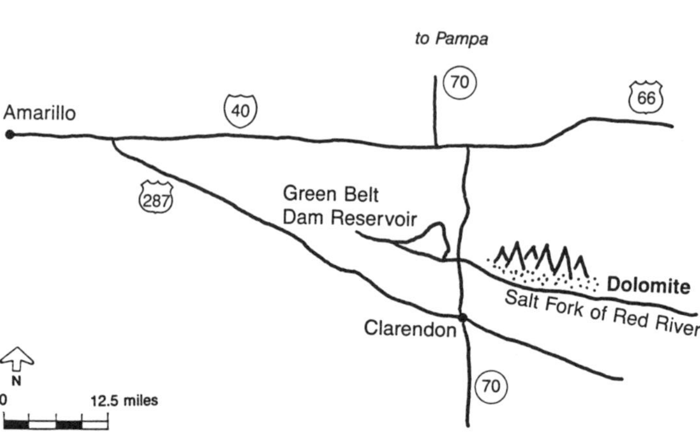

Dolomite is abundant. There are large examples as well as smaller ones suitable for collecting. Along the bottom of the hill in the red sandy soil are rocks that appear to be sandy red in color. If you break one with a hammer, the white dolomite is visible. The outside has simply taken on the color of the soil.

We also found pitchblende. This dark greenish black rock is dense and hard with a dull luster.

Quartz also occurs in massive formations as well as in crystals.

Dolomite from Green Belt Reservoir area.

POINTS OF INTEREST

ALIBATES NATIONAL MONUMENT

Located about 30 miles north of Amarillo on Highway 136, these flint quarries supplied the material for tools and weapons since the time of ancient inhabitants. Though it is no longer open as a collection site, the National Park Service conducts tours daily during the tourist season.

This is where the famous Alibates Flint is found.

PALO DURO CANYON STATE PARK

Located about 12 miles east of Canyon on Highway 217 and Park Road 5, Palo Duro is Texas' largest state park. Magnificent spires and pinnacles top canyon walls which plunge a thousand feet to the floor. This impressive formation was carved by the Red River. It is a must for every rock lover to see, but remember, no collecting.

Palo Duro Canyon is Texas' largest state park, and although rock collecting is off limits, it is a must-see for every rock lover.

Section 4

EAST TEXAS

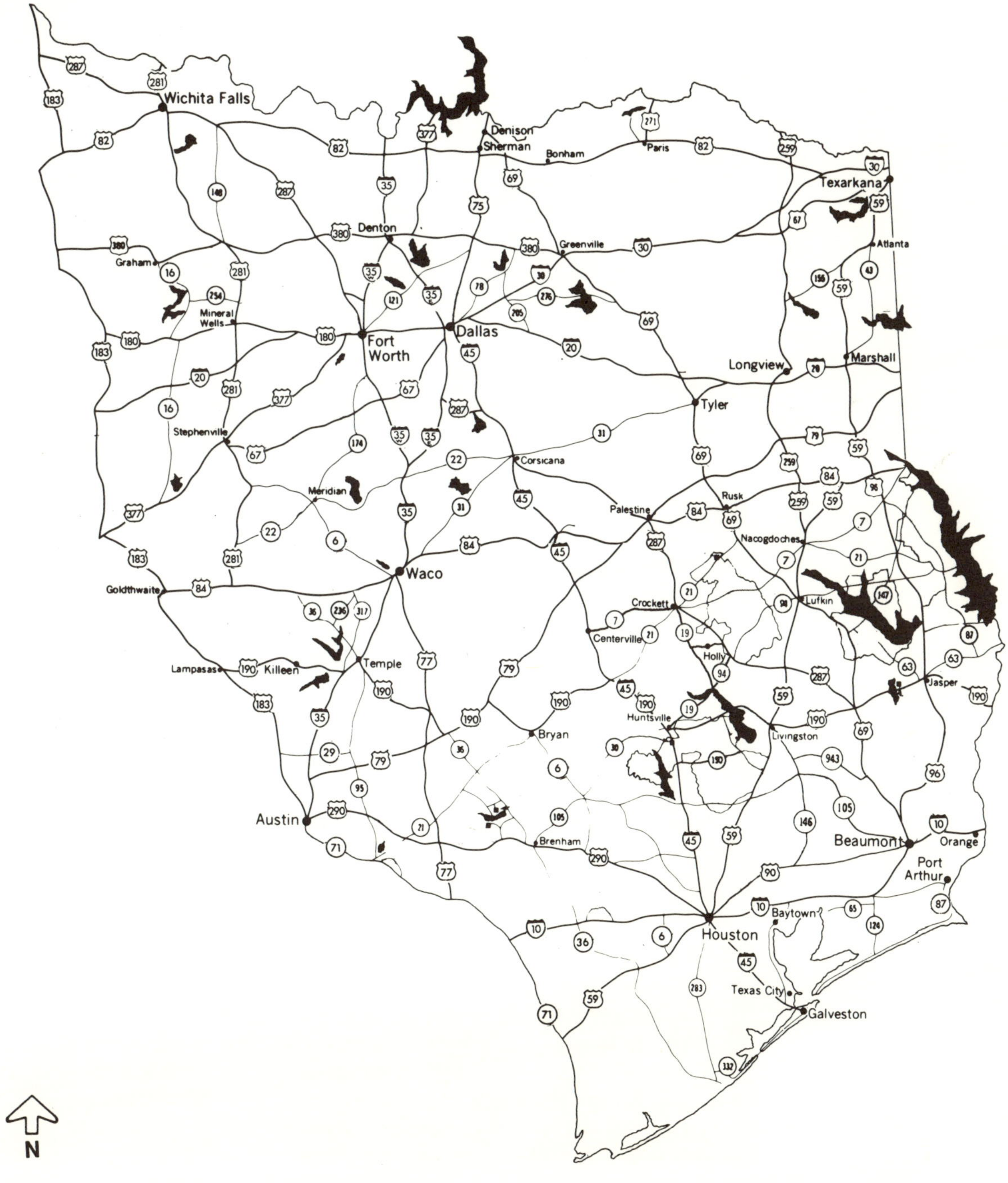

INTRODUCTION

This area of the state is unique from the rest of Texas. It consists mainly of huge volumes of clay and sand deposited during the upper Cretaceous and lower Tertiary periods from 100 to 400 million years ago as the shoreline retreated to its present position.

On the west it is bordered by Highway 183. The rolling black hills of North Texas change to the red iron-bearing sandy soil of East Texas. Traveling south the sparser vegetation turns to the heavily forested piney woods and finally to the sandy beaches of the coast.

In familiar landmarks the area is bordered on the north by the Red River, on the west by a line from Vernon through Brownwood and Austin to the coast, on the south by the Gulf of Mexico and on the east by the state border with Louisiana.

The coastal plains of the southern part of the state are covered with the recent Quarternary sands deposited three million years ago. In other words, this area is covered by soil and sands on the surface and there are no outcroppings of rocks.

Consequently, most of the rocks found in the area are from the older Tertiary soils that start just north of Houston and extend up to Texarkana. This surface formation dates from 70 million years ago. Much of the area's material is seen in washes where the soil has been eroded and the rocks have been carried along in rivers and streams. Even though this fact makes finding the rocks more difficult, the search is very satisfying.

CHALCEDONY

As described earlier this material is the cryptocrystalline variety of quartz that occurs so abundantly around the state.

In East Texas it takes several interesting forms. As also described earlier in this book, the varietal name is defined by the coloring of the material.

The chalcedony most often found here is of the *jasper* variety and occurs in dark red and yellow as rounded weathered rocks in stream beds approximately one to two inches in diameter.

Being very dense and hard with an even smooth texture, this jasper makes wonderful cutting material.

HALITE

This mineral is made up of sodium chloride, or common table salt. It is usually white or colorless, but with natural trace minerals it can be tinted red, blue, gray, brown or green. Rubbed across a streak plate, the mark will be white.

Halite has three directions of cleavage that leave a cube shape to the mineral. This can even be seen by examining table salt with a magnifying glass.

Salt occurs on the Gulf Coastal Plains in huge salt domes that are almost circular in shape, some being more than two miles wide. These domes pushed their way upwards toward the surface from deeply buried halite deposits. It is mined at the Hockley dome in Harris County and the Grand Saline dome in Van Zandt County.

LIMONITE

This is not really one mineral, but a mixture of several creating an iron ore. It has a dull, clay-like luster with a brownish-yellow or rusty brown clay color.

The East Texas Limonite has been mined off and on from about 1855 in open pits.

It has been used also as a building material in some areas. All of the cabins at Caddo Lake were constructed of the ore when built by the WPA in the 1930s.

Red jasper.

Limonite is a mixture of several minerals that form an iron ore.

PETRIFIED WOOD AND PETRIFIED PALM

These materials are pseudomorphs, or false forms, of other substances and are made up of cryptocrystalline quartz or chalcedony. In the process of petrification, quartz has taken over the living cells of the material without distracting from the shape or pattern.

In other words, petrified wood still looks like wood, still has the texture and grain of wood, but is no longer a living form. Instead, it is quartz.

The trace minerals in the living substances add bright and beautiful colors to the petrified wood, but most of the material found in Texas is in shades of brown like the wood itself. Often, it is found with the outer bark pattern still visible and in quite large pieces.

In a great many areas of East Texas, petrified wood has been used as a building material.

Petrified palm is found as small rocks with rounded edges. It is almost always a light cream color, and has the appearance of a solidified sponge, full of minute holes. Having been a very porous wood, it is a very porous rock.

Of the specimens we found only the petrified wood would be suitable for cutting and polishing, as the petrified palm is much too porous and brittle and is best left as specimens.

Petrified wood is a pseudomorph, or false form, in which quartz has replaced the living cells of the wood.

The trace minerals in the living substance add bright and beautiful color to the petrified wood.

Petrified palm.

Some petrified palm is too porous and brittle to be suitable for cutting and polishing.

Petrified wood from Holly Cemetery Road.

SULFUR

Sulfur is not only a mineral but also an element and occurs in purest form as transparent to translucent and yellow in color, but can take on shades of green, brown or red with other minerals. It is soft enough to be scratched with a copper penny and leaves a streak of white or light yellow.

Since sulfur will burn at a low temperature it has the nickname of "brimstone."

One of the best sources of sulfur in Texas is in the southeast where it accompanies the salt domes. It is found in the caprock that sits atop the salt. Since much of the sulfur is found 1500 to 2400 feet below the surface, a new mining method had to be developed for getting it out of the ground. For this, the advantage of a low melting temperature of sulfur was used to best advantage. In this process, superheated water is forced down a pipe to melt the sulfur, then air under high pressure forces it up through another pipe where it is carried to the surface to solidify or be transported as a liquid through a pipeline.

Only on rare occasions is this material found on the surface in crystal form.

EAST TEXAS COLLECTION SITES

CROCKETT AREA

Follow Highway 19 south for 14 miles from Crockett to Lovelady, then go east on 1280 toward Holly. There are many cemetery roads in this area and we found good specimens of petrified wood just lying in the roads. The rocks will sometimes still have patterns of the bark visible. One of the best pieces we found was seen by the side of the road from the car. Another piece had a curved wood grain to it and could have easily been mistaken for a piece of modern wood, but picking it up, the petrification was obvious.

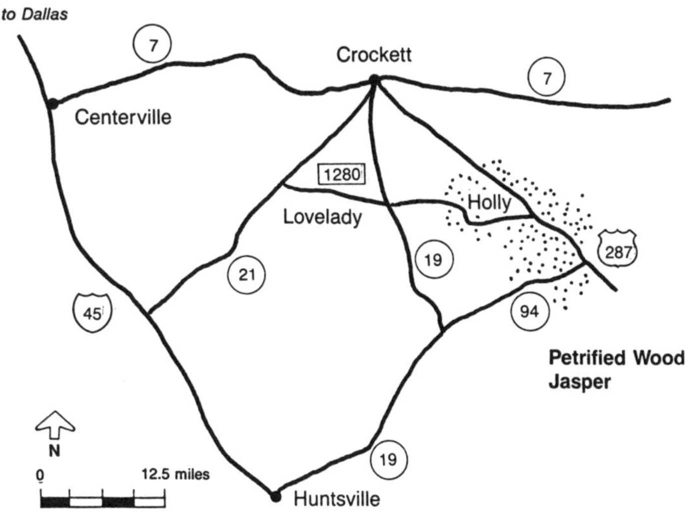

Holly Cemetery Road.

Along a creek bed near the Holly Cemetery Road, we found small pieces of jasper and the ever-present quartz, in half-dollar size stones.

CANEY CREEK

Continue east from Site 1 on 1280 until it runs into Highway 287 at the Davy Crockett National Forest. Go south to Highway 94, then west toward Trinity. Along the banks of Caney Creek, samples of petrified wood, petrified palm and multi-colored jasper are easily accessible if there hasn't been recent rain.

Caney Creek is a good area to collect samples of petrified wood, petrified palm, and multi-colored jasper.

CADDO LAKE-JEFFERSON

On almost any road in this area, the principal type of rock is an iron ore material, limonite. Heavy and reddish brown in color, it has been used frequently as a building material.

POINTS OF INTEREST

CADDOAN MOUNDS

Located between Crockett and Alto on Highway 21, these excavated ruins are the remains of one of Texas' oldest civilizations. There is an informative film presentation and artifact exhibit in the visitor center. There is an admission fee.

MISSION TEJAS STATE HISTORICAL PARK

Located 21 miles northeast of Crockett on Highway 21, this park is in the Davy Crockett National Forest. There is an authentic log home dating from 1828 and a mission replica as well as camping facilities and nature hiking trails.

CADDO LAKE STATE PARK

Two miles north of Highway 43 near Karnack (northeast of Marshall), this park has large specimens of the iron ore common to the area. Since it is a state park, there is no collecting allowed, but the park buildings are examples of the type of building done with this material.

DINOSAUR VALLEY STATE PARK

Five miles west of Glen Rose on Highway 67 and FM 205, this area contains the best preserved dinosaur tracks in Texas. Millions of years ago, some dinosaur walked in the limy mud and its tracks are now preserved in limestone for us to see today. There is an admission fee.

GLOSSARY

Adamantine. "Diamond-like" referring to luster. Adamantine is the highest on the luster scale. Only a diamond possesses an adamantine luster, since, to achieve it, the material must have extreme hardness and brilliance.

Adularescence. The billowy blue light effect of moonstone, a variety of feldspar.

Agate. A commonly used word for different types of chalcedony. Can vary widely in color, pattern, and transparency. It can be found throughout the state.

Almandite. One of a group of garnets, dark red-brown in color, which often occurs with other substances, such as quartz.

Amethyst. A variety of crystalline quartz that is a pale to dark purple color.

Amorphous. Having no form. Material that has no regular arrangement of atoms, and therefore, no crystal structure.

Asbestos. Name given to a group of minerals that form in slender fibers that can be pulled apart. It is used for fire-retardant garments and insulation.

Balcones Fault. A fault that runs through the central portion of Texas.

Barite. Barium sulfate mineral, has a glassy or pearly luster.

Basalt. A dark brown or black igneous rock of feldspar and pyroxene. Used as road building material.

Batholith. A rough mass of igneous rock that has pushed up through several strata to below the surface and then uncovered due to erosion.

Cabochon. A type of gemstone cut with a flat bottom and domed top. Opals are most often cut "en cabochon."

Calcite. Calcium carbonate. A common mineral that often combines with other minerals to form rocks.

Calyx. The floral bud portion of the crinoid, once a sea lily, now seen in fossils in Central Texas.

Cassiterite. Tin dioxide. A primary source of tin. Often found mixed with other minerals.

Cenozoic. The current era on the geologic time scale. It began 63 million years ago.

Chalcedony. The technical name for cryptocrystalline quartz. This common material forms in numerous shapes and colors. Other names for chalcedony: agate, jasper, flint.

Chalk. A fine-grained variety of limestone that is soft enough to leave a mark on surfaces.

Cinnabar. A reddish crystalline ore of mercury, mercury sulfide.

Cleavage. The ability of a material to separate along a certain plane, where the atomic structure is weaker. When broken along a cleavage plane, the surface is flat and sheer.

Cleavage Fragment. A piece of mineral that has cleaved from its parent.

Conchoidal. Shell-like fracture exhibited by most transparent materials that don't have a cleavage property.

Conglomerate. A rock made up of cemented rock or mineral fragments that are mostly gravel size.

Coral. The skeleton of certain marine animals. It commonly forms in branch-like shapes. In Texas, it is found fossilized.

Crinoids. Prehistoric sea animal, called the "sea lily." Now found fossilized in Central Texas.

Cryptocrystalline. A type of crystalline formation where the individual crystals are so small that they cannot be seen, even with a regular microscope. The shape of the formation is massive.

Crystal Habit. The outer shape that the crystal takes. For example, diamond forms in the cubic crystal system, but its habit is octohedron (or some variation thereof).

Crystal System. One of six groups of patterns in which mineral growth occurs.

Crystalline. Having a defined, orderly internal structure.

Crystallization. The orderly arrangement of atoms in minerals according to one of the six crystal systems.

Dendritic. Tree-like formation in mineral growth.

Dolomite. A mineral of calcium-magnesium carbonate, but also a rock of white color with a pearly luster. Found in North Texas.

Dull. A luster that exhibits very little gloss.

Effervescence. The ability of a substance to bubble when exposed to certain chemicals. Example: substances with a carbonate base will effervesce when exposed to a few drops of dilute hydrochloric acid.

Element. Any chemical substance that cannot be further divided into other substances. The building blocks of chemistry. All rocks and minerals are made up of one or more elements.

Extrusive. Igneous rocks that formed by cooling magma that forced its way through the earth's surface.

Fault. A break in the earth's crust along which movement and slippage occur.

Feldspar. A group of similar non-metallic minerals each being aluminum silicate. Fairly hard, but has two directions of cleavage.

Flint. A cryptocrystalline variety of quartz, chalcedony. This material is hard, smooth and even-textured. Used by Indians for arrowheads and hand axes.

Fluorite. Calcium fluoride. A soft, glassy mineral that has four directions of perfect cleavage.

Fossils. The preserved remains of organic substances, plants and animals.

Fracture. The breaking of a substance across the grain. The appearance can be dull, grainy, glassy, conchoidal, splintery.

Galena. Lead sulfide. A metallic, heavy mineral that is a source of lead.

Garnet. A group of minerals that are similar, aluminum silicates. Grossularite and almandite occur in Texas.

Gemstone. A mineral substance that possesses sufficient hardness, beauty and rarity to make it a worthwhile stone to be worn as jewelry.

Geode. A rounded ball-shape boulder, that, when cracked open, shows crystal growth radiating toward the center. Most geodes contain crystals of quartz or calcite.

Gneiss. A metamorphic rock that forms in light and dark bands. Made up of quartz and feldspar.

Granite. A rock that is formed of feldspar, quartz, and sometimes hornblende. Crystallization of the components often visible. Granite is used commonly as building material.

Graphite. The element carbon. A very soft, black mineral with a greasy feel. Same substance as diamond.

Grossularite. One of the two species of garnet found in Texas. An aluminum silicate.

Halite. Sodium chloride, or common table salt. Found in Texas in large domes.

Hardness. The resistance of a substance to scratching or abrasion.

Hematite. Iron oxide; the chief ore of iron. Very heavy with a metallic luster.

Igneous. Rocks that have formed by the cooling of molten rock or magma.

Inorganic. Not pertaining to organic materials, plants and animals. Rocks are inorganic.

Intrusive. Igneous rocks that formed below the earth's surface. Sometimes, through a process of erosion, these reach the surface.

Jasper. A variety of chalcedony, cryptocrystalline quartz that is so common around the state. It is massive in formation and is usually red, yellow or orange.

Limestone. A sedimentary rock, made up mostly of calcite containing grains of other substances. White in pure form, it has been transformed to a limestone state due to pressure from the earth's activity.

Limonite. A mixture of several minerals creating an iron ore. Found in East Texas.

Llanite. A fine-grained pink granite found only in Llano County in Central Texas.

Llano Uplift. Area of Central Texas where Precambrian and early Paleozoic rocks occur. Characterized by intrusive igneous rocks that through weathering and an uplifting process from below the earth's surface are now exposed.

Loupe. A small hand held magnifying device. Usually 10 power.

Luster. The reflective quality of a substance's surface. Brightness.

Magma. Molten rock. When the earth heats rocks to the boiling point, they expand and flow, either below the earth's surface, or through the earth's crust.

Marble. A rock formed of calcite or dolomite that has been recrystallized into a fairly hard material by extreme heat and pressure from below the earth's surface. Used as building material.

Massive. A type of rock formation characterized by its boulder appearance, as opposed to a crystal shape.

Mesozoic. An era on the geologic time scale beginning 230 million years ago and ending 63 million years ago.

Metallic. Luster having the reflective qualities of metal.

Metamorphic. A type of rock that has gone through a change. In geologic terms, metamorphic rock is that which has undergone a change from the original, usually because of exposure to heat, pressure and gases generated below the earth's surface to form a new substance.

Mica. A group of potassium-aluminum silicate minerals that form with a cleavage plane so distinct that the substance can be separated into thin sheets. Extremely heat resistant.

Microcline. One of the groups of feldspars.

Mineral. An inorganic chemical substance made up of one or more elements. Can sometimes have an organic origin, as in the case of coal.

Mohs Scale. Standard scale of hardness used in both mineralogy and gemology.

Obsidian. Naturally occurring volcanic glass; made up of feldspar and quartz.

Opal. A non-crystalline or amorphous silicate material. Sometimes exhibits "play of color."

Opaque. Allowing absolutely no light to penetrate.

Organic. Living or once living substances. Organic materials are characterized by their ability to decay.

Orthoclase. One of the varieties of feldspar that is found in Texas.

Outcroppings. The projection of layers of rock above the surface.

Overburden. Term used to describe the overhang of earth when the lower surface has been removed, either by nature or by man.

Paleozoic. An era on the geologic time scale that began 600 million years ago and ended 230 million years ago.

Pearly. A luster resembling the soft shimmer of a pearl.

Petrified Wood and Petrified Palm. The result of quartz material having taken over the structure of either palm or wood. It is really chalcedony, but still retains the grain of wood or palm.

Pitchblende. A dark mineral of uranium dioxide, with submetallic luster and no crystal shape.

Precambrian. An era on the geologic time scale that ended some 600 million years ago.

Pseudomorph. Pseudo = false, morph = form. Occasionally, one substance takes over another, but retains the characteristics of the original. Petrified wood is an example of this. In reality it is chalcedony, a cryptocrystalline variety of quartz, but it has the graining of the wood.

Pyrite. A bright, yellow, metallic mineral. Iron disulfide. Dubbed "fool's gold" for its visual resemblance to gold.

Quarternary. The current period of the Cenozoic geologic scale. We are in it now and it has lasted for the past one million years.

Quartz (Silicon Dioxide). A very commonly occurring mineral in the state of Texas and around the world. Can take several forms ranging from hexagonally shaped crystals to cryptocrystalline masses.

Root. Also called the "holdfast," this portion of the crinoid secures the sea lily to the sea bed. Now seen only in fossil form in limestone.

Salt Domes. Giant pillars of naturally occurring salt that have formed under the earth's surface.

Sandstone. Grains of sand that have been cemented together in a natural process to form a stone. Usually made up of quartz grains.

Sedimentary. Rock formation resulting from the building up of sediments that, over a period of many centuries, become cemented together.

Selenite. A colorless, glassy, transparent variety of gypsum. It is soft, brittle and has one direction of perfect cleavage. Found in crystalline form in North Texas.

Serpentine. Can be a rock or mineral. Hydrous magnesium silicate with layered or fibrous formation. Sometimes used as building material.

Silver. An element as well as a mineral. White metal that, along with gold and platinum, is considered a precious metal and is used for making jewelry. It is often found in conjunction with other minerals.

Spalling. The process of splitting or breaking away of stone. Usually caused by earth's movement or erosion. Creates a domed shape rock. Enchanted Rock exhibits this process.

Specific Gravity. The density of a material, the compactness of the molecules. The specific gravity of water is 1. It is the ratio of a substance's weight in air divided by the weight in air less the weight in water.

Stalactites. An icicle-like formation hanging from the roof of a cavern caused by the flow of lime-laden water over a surface, where it comes out of solution and remains as sedimentary rock.

Stalagmites. Cone like formations on cavern floors. Made up of the same material as stalactites.

Stem. The stalk portion of crinoids.

Streak. Characteristic color left when a mineral or rock is rubbed across a streak plate or tile.

Submetallic. A luster slightly duller than metallic.

Sulfur. A mineral as well as an element, usually found as a yellow to reddish yellow translucent massive substance. Used to manufacture sulfuric acid.

Talc. An extremely soft mineral of hydrous magnesium silicate. It possesses a perfect cleavage property and is number 1 on the hardness scale.

Tectile. Able to be cut through with a knife.

Tertiary. The first portion of the Cenozoic geologic period. It lasted 62 million years.

Topaz. An aluminum fluorosilicate mineral that forms in colorless to pale blue crystals in Texas. It has a high specific gravity and is hard, but possesses a perfect basal cleavage property. Found in central Texas.

Topography. The physical features of a region.

Tourmaline. Complex silicate of boron and aluminum. In fine clear crystals it is used as a gemstone, but that occurring in Texas is black (schorl) and brown (dravite) and not suitable for gemstones.

Translucent. Allowing light to pass through, but not allowing objects to be distinguished. An example of this is frosted glass.

Transparent. Allowing light to pass through so that an object can be seen.

Vitreous. A luster that is glassy.

Volcanic. Materials that have their origin as a result of the earth's surface eruption.

Waxy. A luster that has the appearance of wax.

TEXAS GEM AND MINERAL CLUBS

Arlington Gem and Mineral Club
P.O. Box 170175
Arlington, TX 76003

Austin Gem and Mineral Society, Inc.
P.O. Box 4327
Austin, TX 78765-4327

Big Spring Prospector's Club, Inc.
P.O. Box 1182
Big Spring, TX 79720

Central Texas Gem and Mineral Society, Inc.
401 First State Bank Bldg.
Abilene, TX 79602

Clear Lake Gem and Mineral Society, Inc.
P.O. Box 58072
Houston, TX 77258

Cross Timbers Gem and Mineral Club
Rt. 3, Box 190-B
Dublin, TX 76446

Dallas Gem and Mineral Society, Inc.
4104 Southwestern Blvd.
Dallas, TX 75225

East Texas Gem and Mineral Society
2608 Oak Lane
Tyler, TX 75701

Faceters' Guild
3202 Boyd
Midland, TX 79705

Fort Worth Gem and Mineral Club
3545 Bryan Ave.
Fort Worth, TX 76110

Fredericksburg Rockhounds
P.O. Box 231
Fredericksburg, TX 78624

Galveston County Gem and Mineral Society
728 Hackberry
La Marque, TX 77568

Golden Spread Gem and Mineral Society
P.O. Box 19144
Amarillo, TX 79114

Graham Gem and Mineral Club
Murray Rd.
Graham, TX 76046

Gulf Coast Gem and Mineral Society, Inc.
P.O. Box 6494, Lamar Station
Corpus Christi, TX 78411

Highland Lakes Gem and Mineral Society
P.O. Box 490
Kingsland, TX 78639

Hi-Plains Rock Club
200 NE Alpine
Plainview, TX 79072

Houston Gem and Mineral Society
P.O. Box 492
Bellaire, TX 77401

Houston Lapidary Society
P.O. Box 6601
Houston, TX 77265

Kerr County Gem and Mineral Society
24 Yucca
Kerrville, TX 78028

Lubbock Gem and Mineral Society
P.O. Box 6371
Lubbock, TX 79413

Magic Valley Gem and Mineral Society
Rt. 4, Box 910, Lot #24
Edinburg, TX 78539

Mineral Moochers of Brazoria County
Box 307
Angleton, TX 77515

Oak Cliff Gem and Mineral Society
502 Ogden St.
Dallas, TX 75211

Pasadena Gem and Mineral Society
Box 847
Pasadena, TX 77501

Pleasant Oaks Gem and Mineral Club
8723 Santa Clara
Dallas, TX 75218

Rollin' Rock Club, Inc.
Star Rt.
Henrietta, TX 76365

Sabine Neches Gem and Mineral Society
P.O. Box 1624
Beaumont, TX 77704

Southwest Gem and Mineral Society, Inc.
P.O. Box 12530
San Antonio, TX 78212

Texas Faceter's Guild
6503 Almeda Rd.
Houston, TX 77021

Texoma Rockhounds, Inc.
1600 West Hull Street
Denison, TX 75020

Tri-City Gem and Mineral Society, Inc.
P.O. Box 735
Temple, TX 76503

Twin Cities Mineralogical Society
P.O. Box 5966
Texarkana, TX 75501

Victoria Gem and Mineral Society
P.O. Box 3078
Victoria, TX 77903

Waco Gem and Mineral Club
1812 N. 15th St.
Waco, TX 76703

Williamson County Gem and Mineral Society
P.O. Box 441
Georgetown, TX 78626

BIBLIOGRAPHY

Girard, Roselle M., *Texas Rocks and Minerals—An Amateur's Guide*, Bureau of Economic Geology, 1964.

Liddicoat Jr., Richard T., *Handbook of Gem Identification*, Gemological Institute of America, 1972.

Matthews III, William H., *Texas Fossils—An Amateur Collector's Handbook*, Bureau of Economic Geology, 1960.

Parsons, Charles J., *Practical Gem Knowledge for the Amateur*, Lapidary Journal, Inc., 1969.

Simpson, Bessie W., *Gem Trails of Texas*, Gem Guides Book Co., 1981.

SURFACE GEOLOGY OF TEXAS

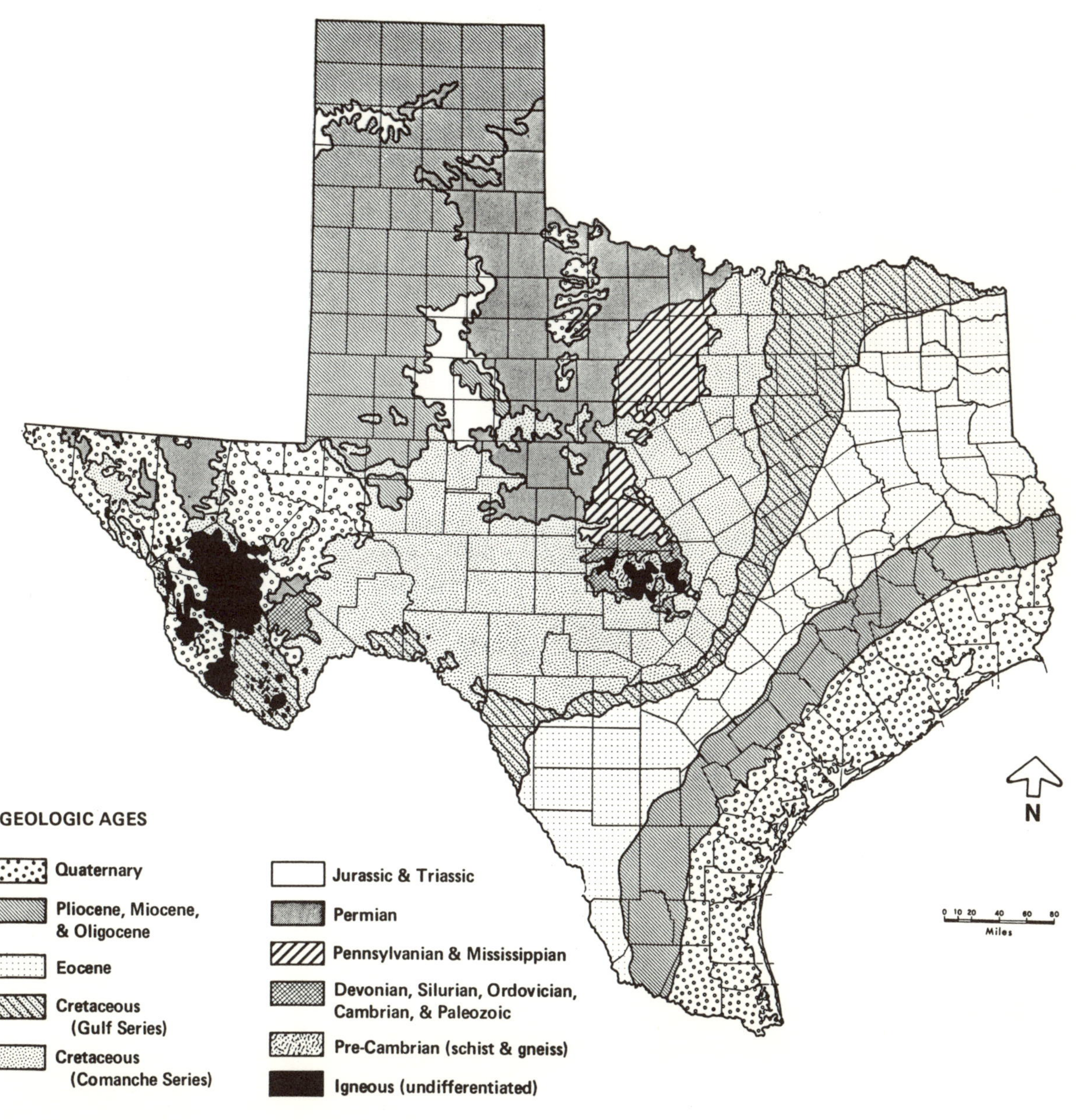

Source: Bureau of Economic Geology, The University of Texas, 'Geologic Map of Texas.'

INDEX